OUR VICTORY OVER DEATH:
RESURRECTION?

Our Victory Over Death: Resurrection?

Marie-Emile Boismard

translated by
Madeleine Beaumont

A Liturgical Press Book

 THE LITURGICAL PRESS
Collegeville, Minnesota

This book was originally published in French under the title *Faut-il encore parler de "résurrection"?* © 1995 by Les Éditions du Cerf.

Cover design by David Manahan, O.S.B. Illustration: Der Verduner Altar, detail: *The Dead Arise;* 14th cent., Klosterneuburg, Austria.

The Scripture quotations, unless otherwise specified, are from the New Revised Standard Version Bible, Catholic edition, © 1993 and 1989 by the Division of Christian Education of the National Council of the Churches of Christ in the U.S.A. Used by permission. All rights reserved.

1	2	3	4	5	6	7	8

Library of Congress Cataloging-in-Publication Data

Boismard, M. E.
    [Faut-il encore parler de résurrection?   English]
    Our victory over death : resurrection? / Marie-Emile Boismard ; Madeleine Beaumont, translator.
        p.   cm.
    Includes bibliographical references and indexes.
    ISBN 0-8146-2458-8 (alk. paper)
    1. Resurrection–Biblical teaching.   2. Immortality–Biblical teaching. I. Title.
BS680.R37B6513   1998
236'.8–dc21
        98-29486
        CIP

Contents

Part Three
The Risen Christ

Conclusion

Foreword

Tuesday, April 8, 1963. Petra, magical and tragic. A group of twenty-five persons, guided by Jean Steinman, curate at Notre-Dame de Paris, is about to enter the Siq, the narrow defile leading to the city, enclosed between its cliffs of rose sandstone. A torrential downpour. Brutally, a *seid*, a flash flood, carries away almost the entire group in its roaring waters. Only two persons escape death.

Two days later, in the military hospital in Amman. The bodies are lined up in a hall, at least those which the Jordanian army has retrieved so far. Their forms are glimpsed under the white sheets. The two survivors are there to identify the victims. One of them asks me, "Steinman used to tell us that people rise immediately after death; is it true?" The question takes me by surprise because I have never seriously thought about the problem. I have been content to hold what I was always taught: at death, our soul leaves its body, but it will be reunited with it when the general resurrection occurs at the end of time. Christ will come down from heaven to accomplish this great mystery. Therefore, I give my questioner a prudent, if evasive, answer. A few weeks later, I receive an insistent letter urging me to answer the question put to me. The only thing I can do is research the texts of biblical revelation, and I set about my work at once.

Five different times during the following decades, "Our victory over Death" was the subject I took for my course at the Ecole biblique in Jerusalem. It was also the topic I developed for five weeks at the Jesuits' Pontifical Biblical Institute in Rome. Besides, the very same subject was what I taught in the seminary Redemptoris Mater in Takamatsu, Japan. The present book contains the results of my research.

Very early on, I became convinced that no text from either the Old or New Testament speaks of the resurrection of the *body* (in the Greek philosophical meaning of the word) when Christ returns at the end of time. This is true even of chapter 15 from 1 Corinthians. In fact, I observed that from the second century B.C.E. on, even though the Bible states that the end of our earthly life does not mean the end of our human destiny, the ways of envisioning "our victory over death" are different. First, there is the "resurrection" current, which uses the terms of a Semitic anthropology that makes no distinction between soul and body. It is the whole person who will come back to life. The language employed here is that of the resurrection of the *dead,* and not just of their bodies. This is the theme which we find developed in the prophet Daniel and 2 Maccabees and in Paul's first letter to the Thessalonians and first letter to the Corinthians. Second, there is the "immortality" current, which borrows ideas from Greek philosophy: at death, only the body disintegrates whereas the soul does not die because it is immortal. This theme, however, is developed in two different ways. The first is found in the book of Wisdom; according to its author, influenced by Platonic philosophy, the souls of the righteous are led to God after sojourning in Hades for a period of time. There is no question of their being joined again with their bodies. The second way is found in Paul; in 2 Corinthians, Paul modifies Platonism by means of Semitic realism. According to him, at the time of death, the souls of the righteous leave their bodies behind and rejoin Christ in God's presence; but they immediately find celestial bodies waiting for them in heaven. This was, I believe, also the thinking of Jesus, although he expressed himself with less clarity. (This was an unexpected discovery for me!)

Therefore, here are the conclusions of my research. From the biblical point of view, one must distinguish the *fact* and the *how* of our victory over death. God affirms that God will not abandon us to the power of death, and we must believe this. But how will this victory over death be realized? The answer to this question is not part of revelation since the Bible offers us several solutions. Thus it is no longer a problem of revelation, but one of philosophy and therefore of theology because theology interprets biblical data by means of a specific philosophy.

If, owing to philosophical reflection or personal intuition, one believes that our final destiny is fixed at the end of our earthly life without any need to wait until the end of time and the return of Christ, this opinion can be supported by what Paul (in his second phase) wrote to the faithful of Corinth, and even, it seems, by what Jesus had taught his disciples. This is the answer that I feel myself able to give today to the question put to me two days after the Petra catastrophe.

The question of our victory over death is linked with that of the eschatological world in which we will live once death has been definitively vanquished. On this point also, the study of the texts gave me some surprises. For example, I realized that Paul's thought had evolved. Following the prophet Daniel, he had first accepted that our eschatological destiny would unfold on earth, albeit a somewhat idealized earth. Later on, he imagined a world of light, similar to that of the stars in the sky. Only at the end of his life did he place our beatific vision in God.

Before inviting readers to follow me into the analysis of the texts, I must make clear an important point. To understand divine revelation concerning our victory over death, which was a gradual process, we must not single out a specific passage but take into account the whole of the texts presented to us, a principle on which all theologians agree. As a consequence, we must not be surprised, still less scandalized, to discover, for instance, that the author of the book of Wisdom, like Plato, does not envision any resurrection of the body. Similarly, we should not find it surprising that Paul came to change his position because, enlightened by the Spirit, he gained a better understanding of the real dimensions of the issue. By the way, I found Paul more congenial (I do prefer John, less obsessed by the problem of sin) on the day I discovered that he was afraid of death, even though he was certain he would join Christ upon taking leave of his body. In spite of everything, does not death entail a tearing apart of our being?

I am adding a last remark. All the texts which we are going to peruse have been abundantly discussed by exegetes. In order to avoid overloading this book, I have reduced the bibliographical references, especially the French ones, to the essential. Should certain exegetes be disappointed, I refer them to the first volume of the monumental work of Emile Puech on the belief in the resurrection among the Essenes of Qumran. I do not always agree with his conclusions, especially those concerning the New Testament texts, but I can only bow to the erudition he displays. Scholars in exegesis will find there a documentation which should, I think, give them satisfaction.

List of Abbreviations

Alfrink, "L'idée" : Alfrink, Bernard J. "L'idée de résurrection d'après Dan 12,2." *Bibl.* 40 (1959) 355–371.

Barucq, "O salmo 49" : Barucq, André. "O salmo e o livro de Qohelet." *Atualidades Biblicas.* Ed. S. Voigt and Fr. Vier, 297–308. Petropolis, 1971.

Bauer–Aland, *Wörterbuch* : Bauer, Walter. *Griechisch-deutches Wörterbuch zu den Schriften des Neuen Testaments und der frühchristlichen Literatur,* 6th ed, rev. Ed. Kurt and Barbara Aland. New York, 1988.

BJ : Bible de Jérusalem.

Bibl. : *Biblica.*

Black, *Apocalypsis* : Black, Matthew, ed. *Apocalypsis Henochi Graece.* Fragmenta Pseudepigraphorum, quae supersunt Graeca. Pseudepigrapha Veteris Testamenti Graece 3. Leiden, 1970.

Black, *Enoch* : Black, Matthew, ed. *The Book of Enoch, or, I Enoch.* In consultation with James C. Vanderkam. Studia in Veteris Testamenti Pseudepigrapha 7. Leiden, 1985.

Boismard, *Marc* : Boismard, Marie-Emile. *L'évangile de Marc: Sa préhistoire.* Paris, 1994.

Boismard, *Synpose 2* : Boismard, Marie-Emile. *Commentaire.* Collaboration of Arnaud Lamouille and Pierre Sandevoir. *Synopse des quatre évangiles en français.* Ed. Paul Benoit and Marie-Emile Boismard. Vol. 2. Paris, 1980.

Boismard–Lamouille, *Synopse 3* : *L'évangile de Jean.* Collaboration of G. Rochais. *Synopse des quatre évangiles en français.* Ed. Paul Benoit and Marie-Emile Boismard. Vol. 3. Paris, 1977.

CBQ : *Catholic Biblical Quarterly.*

Charles, *Enoch* : Charles, Robert H., ed. *The Book of Enoch or I Enoch.* Trans. from the ed.'s Ethiopic text; introduction, notes, and indexes wholly recast, enlarged and rewritten. Jerusalem, 1973.

Cullmann, *Immortalité* : Cullmann, Oscar. *Immortalité de l'âme ou Résurrection des morts? Le témoignage du Nouveau Testament*. L'actualité protestant. Neuchâtel, 1956.

Dahl, *Resurrection* : Dahl, Murdoch E. *The Resurrection of the Body: A Study of I Corinthians 15*. Studies in Biblical Theology 36. Naperville, Ill., 1962.

Deissmann, *Licht* : Deissmann, Gustav A. *Licht vom Osten: Das neue Testament und die neuentdeckten Texte der hellenistisch-römische Welt*, 4th ed. Tübingen, 1923.

Dhorme, "Le séjour" : Dhorme, Paul. "Le séjour des morts chez les Babyloniens et les Hébreux." *RB* 4 (1907) 59–78.

Dreyfus, "L'argument" : Dreyfus, P. "L'argument scriptuaraire de Jésus en faveur de la résurrection des morts." *RB* 66 (1959) 213–224.

Dupont, *ΣΥΝ ΧΡΙΣΤΩΙ:* Dupont, Jacques. *ΣΥΝ ΧΡΙΣΤΩΙ: L'union avec le Christ suivant saint Paul*. Bruges, 1952.

Dupont-Sommer, *Le Quatrième* : Dupont-Sommer, André. *Le quatrième livre des Maccabées*. Paris, 1939.

Festugière, *L'idéal* : Festugière, André-Jean. *L'idéal religieux des Grecs et L'Evangile*. Etudes bibliques. Paris, 1932.

Feuillet, "La demeure" : Feuillet, André. "La demeure céleste et la destinée des chrétiens." *RechSR* 44 (1956) 161–192, 360–402.

Frey, "La vie" : Frey, Jean Baptiste. "La vie de l'au-delà dans les conceptions juives au temps de Jésus-Christ." *Bibl.* 13 (1932) 129–168.

Gilbert, "Sagesse" : Gilbert, Maurice. "Sagesse de Salomon (ou Livre de la Sagesse)." *SDB* 11. Paris (1991) cols. 58–119.

Grelot, "La légende" : Grelot, Pierre. "La légende d'Hénoch dans les apocryphes et dans la Bible: Origine et signification." *RechSR* 46 (1958) 5–26, 181–210.

Grelot, "L'eschatologie" : Grelot, Pierre. "L'eschatologie de la Sagesse et les apocalypses juives." *A la rencontre de Dieu: Mémorial Albert Gelin*. Ed. André Barucq, 165–178. Le Puy, 1961.

Grelot, "L'eschatologie des esséniens" : Grelot, Pierre. "L'eschatologie des esséniens et le livre d'Hénoch." *RQ* 1 (1958) 113–131.

Grelot, "Histoire" : Grelot, Pierre. "Histoire et eschatologie dans le livre de Daniel." *Apocalypses et théologie de l'espérance: Congrès de Toulouse (1979)*. Ed. Louis Monloubou. LD 95. Paris, 1977.

Guntermann, *Die Eschatologie* : Guntermann, Friedrich. *Die Eschatologie des Hl. Paulus*. Münster, 1932.

Hadas, *Third Macc* : Hadas, Moses, ed. and trans. *The Third and Fourth Books of Maccabees*. New York, 1953.

HTR : *Harvard Theological Review.*

Johnson, *Vitality* : Johnson, Aubrey R. *The Vitality of the Individual in the Thought of Ancient Israel.* Cardiff, 1964.

Josephus, *Ant.* : Josephus, Flavius. *Antiquities of the Jews. The Works of Flavius Josephus.* Trans. William Whiston. 4 vols. Grand Rapids, Mich., 1974.

Josephus, *War* : Josephus, Flavius. *The Jewish War.* Ed. Gaalya Cornfeld. Grand Rapids, Mich.: 1982.

Knibb, "Martyrdom" : Knibb, Michael A. "Martyrdom and Ascension of Isaiah." *The Old Testament Pseudepigrapha and the New Testament: Prolegomena for the Study of Christian Origins.* Ed. James H. Charlesworth. New York, 1985.

Kübler-Ross, *Les Derniers* : Kübler-Ross, Elisabeth. *Les Derniers Instants de la vie.* Geneva, 1975.

Lagrange, *Mark* : Lagrange, Marie-Joseph, ed. *The Gospel according to Saint Mark.* New York, 1930.

Lambrecht, "Structure" : Lambrecht, Jan. "Structure and Line of Thought in 1 Cor. 15:23-28." *NT* 32 (1990) 143–151.

Larcher, *Etudes* : Larcher, Chrysostome. *Etudes sur le livre de la Sagesse.* Etudes bibliques. Paris, 1969.

Larcher, *Sagesse* : Larcher, Chrysostome. *Le Livre de la Sagesse ou la Sagesse de Salomon.* Etudes bibliques, n.s. 1, 3. Paris, 1983–1984.

LD : Lectio Divina.

Léon-Dufour, "Apparitions" : Léon-Dufour, Xavier. "Apparitions du Ressuscité et herméneutique." *La Résurrection du Christ et l'exégèse moderne.* By P. de Surgy and others. LD 50. Paris, 1969. [*The Resurrection and Modern Biblical Thought.* Trans. Charles Underhill Quinn. New York, 1970.]

Liddell–Scott, *Lexicon* : Liddell, Henry George, and Robert Scott. *A Greek-English Lexicon,* rev. and augm. by Henry Stuart Jones and Roderick McKenzie, 9th ed. New York, 1996.

LV : *Lumière et Vie.*

LXX : Septuagint.

Masset, "Immortalité" : Masset, Pierre. "Immortalité et l'âme, résurrection des corps: Approches philosophiques." *NRT* 105 (1983) 321–344.

Milik, *Books* : Milik, Josef T. *The Books of Enoch: Aramaic Fragments of Qumran Cave 4.* Oxford, 1976.

Milik, "Problèmes" : Milik, Josef T. "Problèmes de la littérature Hénochique à la lumière des fragments araméens de Qumrân." *HRT* 64 (1981) 333–378.

Moingt, "Immortalité" : Moingt, Joseph. "Immortalité de l'âme et/ou résurrection." *LV* 107 (1972) 65–78.

Mollat, "Glory" : Mollat, Donatien. "Glory." *Dictionary of Biblical Theology*. Ed. Xavier Léon-Dufour and others. Trans. under direction of Joseph Cahill. New York, 1967.

Moody, *Life* : Moody, Raymond A. *Life after Life: The Investigation of a Phenomenon–Survival of Bodily Death*. Harrisburg, Penn., 1976.

Moody, *Light* : Moody, Raymond A., with Paul Perry. *The Light Beyond*. New York, 1988.

Nickelsburg, "Apocalyptic" : Nickelsburg, George W. E. "The Apocalyptic Message of 1 Enoch 92–105." *CBQ* 39 (1977) 319.

Nickelsburg, *Resurrection* : Nickelsburg, George, W. E. *Resurrection, Immortality, and Eternal Life in Intertestamental Judaism*, 112–130. Harvard Theological Studies 26. Cambridge, 1972.

NJB: New Jerusalem Bible.

NRT : *Nouvelle revue théologique*.

NT : *Novum Testamentum*.

Philo, *Works* : Philo of Alexandria. *The Works of Philo*. Trans. C.D. Yonge. Peabody, Mass., 1993.

Plato, *Dialogues* : Plato, *Dialogues*. Trans. Benjamin Jowett. Chicago, 1952.

Puech, *La Croyance* : Puech, Emile. *La Croyance des esséniens en la vie future: Immortalité, résurrection, vie éternelle? Histoire d'une croyance dans le judaïsme ancien*. Vol. 1: *La résurrection des morts et le contexte scripturaire*. Etudes bibliques, n.s. 21. Paris, 1993.

RB : *Revue biblique*.

RechSR : *Recherches de science religieuse*.

RQ : *Revue de Qumrân*.

Schillebeeckx, *Church* : Schillebeeckx, Edward. *Church: The Human Story of God*. New York, 1991.

SDB : *Dictionnaire de la Bible, Supplément*. Ed. Louis Pirot and others. Paris, 1928–.

Stemberger, *Der Leib* : Stemberger, Günter. *Der Leib der Auferstehung*. Analecta Biblica 56. Rome, 1972.

Tresmontant, *Study* : Tresmontant, Claude. *A Study of Hebrew Thought*. Trans. Michael Francis Gibson. New York, 1960.

Tromp, *Primitive* : Tromp, Nicholas J. *Primitive Conceptions of Death and the Nether World in the Old Testament*. Biblica et Orientalia 21. Rome, 1969.

TWNT : *Theologisches Wöorterbuch zum Neuen Testament.* Ed. Gerhard Kittel. 10 vols. Stuttgart, 1933–1979. [*Theological Dictionary of the New Testament.* Ed. Gerhard Kittel. Trans. and ed. Geoffrey W. Bromiley. 10 vols. Grand Rapids, Mich., 1964–1976.]

Van Eersel, *La Source* : Van Eersel, Patrice. *La Source noire: Révélations aux portes de la mort.* Paris, 1986.

Part One

THE RESURRECTION
OF THE DEAD

1

The Prophet Daniel

—— (12:1-3) ——

According to an opinion which has gained wide acceptance, the idea of resurrection would have taken shape in Jewish thought only in the beginning of the second century B.C.E. This was in the period of Antiochus Epiphanes' persecution against those who opposed the hellenization of the Jewish people and wanted to safeguard the prescriptions of the Mosaic Law as it was interpreted at the time. Since God is the master and giver of all life, must not God, through love of the elect people, give life back to those who had sacrificed it out of faithfulness? Could those who loved God to the point of dying for God be definitively abandoned? No, God remains faithful to the divine promises. God planned to give life back, at some point in the future, to those who had sacrificed it out of fidelity to the Law. This is what both Daniel and the author of 2 Maccabees affirm.

Although Antiochus Epiphanes does not appear by name in Daniel's book, it is he whom the prophet berates, according to the Jewish historian Flavius Josephus, whose opinion has been generally accepted. The several visions described in Daniel's book aim at comforting God's faithful servants subjected to the tyrant's persecution, by announcing the persecutor's ruin and the restoration of God's people in freedom and faithfulness to the divine law. But, at the time of this "restoration," so ardently desired, what will be the fate of those who, faithful to the Law, will have disappeared from the world of the living? The answer to this agonizing question is given only in the beginning of chapter 12, that is, in the last vision described by the prophet. Here is the translation of this text according to the New Jerusalem Bible;[1] later on, we shall modify it somewhat.

> 1. At that time Michael will arise–the great Prince, defender of your people. That will be a time of great distress, unparalleled since nations first came into existence. When that time comes, your own people will be spared–all those whose names are found written in the Book.
> 2. Of those who are sleeping in the Land of Dust, many will awaken, some to everlasting life, some to shame and everlasting [horror; BJ].
> 3. Those who are wise will shine as brightly as the expanse of the heavens, and those who have instructed many in uprightness, as bright as stars for all eternity.

This text needs explaining in several respects.

The Sources Adopted by Daniel

In the composition of this prophecy, Daniel found inspiration in three texts from the prophet Isaiah, or at least texts which he read in the oracles attributed to Isaiah.

– The first text selected by Daniel is Isaiah 4:2-3. Here is its translation:

> 2. On that day, the branch of the LORD shall be beautiful and glorious, and the fruit of the land shall be the pride and glory of the survivors of Israel.
> 3. Whoever is left in Zion and remains in Jerusalem will be called holy, everyone who has been recorded for life in Jerusalem.

This theme reappears at the end of Daniel 12:1, quoted just above. It refers to those who will still be alive at the time of

---

[1] Biblical references are from the NRSV, except when otherwise indicated. –Ed.

the great eschatological trial. While many will be put to death by the invader, those who are written in the "book of life" will escape the massacre.

– Above, Daniel examines the case of those who will still be alive at the time of the great eschatological trial; but what about those who are already dead? Will not they have a share in the new kingdom? Yes, answers Daniel in verse 2, repeating a text (Isa 26:19) from what is called "the Apocalypse of Isaiah," a late piece of writing which can be dated to the third or fourth centuries B.C.E. Let us give it here in the translation proposed by Emile Puech:

> The dead will live again, the corpses will rise,
> the dwellers in dust will awaken and rejoice,
> because your dew is a dew of light[s]
> and the land of shades will give birth [literally "drop"].[2]

A certain number of the expressions in this text from Isaiah are found again or have their equivalents in Daniel's verse 2: "live again" and "life," "to awaken," "the dwellers in dust," and "those who are sleeping in the Land of Dust." That Daniel borrowed from pseudo-Isaiah is certain. But when pseudo-Isaiah speaks of a resurrection of the dead, does he understand it in the proper and personal sense or in the figurative and collective sense? Will individuals rise again or will the people of God, decimated for a time by their enemies, come back to life (cf. Hos 6:1-2)? The exegetes' opinions are divided on this point. Without going into a thorough discussion of this problem, which is of minor importance for us here, we agree with Puech:[3] "It seems to us that this verse is an undeniable testimony to a belief in a life after death and in a resurrection followed by eschatological joy, a belief already held in some Jewish circles at an early period, antedating Daniel and the Septuagint, which have understood this passage as referring to a bodily resurrection."[4]

---

[2] Puech, *La Croyance,* 70ff.

[3] Ibid., 71.

[4] This adjective seems inappropriate to us because it leads to the supposition of a real distinction between the body and the soul, a

– Lastly, let us note the end of Daniel's verse 2: among those who will rise, some are destined to everlasting horror. This term is taken from Isaiah 66:24 where it is prophesied that the corpses of those who rebelled against God will be "held in horror by all humanity" (NJB). This word is not found anywhere else in the Bible, so the borrowing from Isaiah is more than probable.

It is worth noting these various references to the book of Isaiah because they will enable us to solve some of the difficulties of Daniel's text.

Resurrection of the Body?

When we speak of resurrection, we too often forget that this word does not have exactly the same meaning for us, influenced as we are by an anthropology of Greek origin, and for Daniel, who still adhered to a Semitic anthropology. This is what we now must examine in more detail.

Here is how many people today picture the resurrection to themselves. According to a representation inherited from Platonism, we accept that human beings are composed of a soul and a body, which are two distinct and separate realities. All of our conscious life, that is, intelligence, will, feelings, is concentrated in our soul; the body is only an "instrument" which allows us to come into contact with the external world. Each one of us is above all a soul, but a soul that possesses a body. Whereas the soul is immortal, the body is subject to corruption. Death is the separation of the soul from the body. The body dissolves in the ground, is burned with fire, or even is absorbed by another body, but the soul continues living, either with God or with the fallen angels, whose dire fate it shares. After death, we are nothing but souls separated from their bodies, but still endowed with consciousness and personality since consciousness and personality are the prerogative of the soul. We have shed our bodies like a garment too old and too

---

distinction that Semitic thought did not accept, as we shall see in more detail below.

worn out. We now enjoy eternal bliss with God (let us remain optimistic).

But a day will come, "at the end of time," upon Christ's return, when we shall rejoin our bodies: this will be the resurrection of the body. According to an iconography popularized by famous painters, the graves will open and all the bodies will come out to resume living and to be reunited with the souls that are waiting for them either in heaven or in hell. This is an overly simplistic way of imagining the resurrection since, as anyone knows, there are no longer any "bodies" in the tombs. The physical elements of which they were made have dispersed and been used to form other "bodies." Under these conditions, we must admit that at the general resurrection, there will be as it were a re-creation of bodies by God. Many people today are of this opinion. But in any case, for us nowadays, the term "resurrection," strictly speaking, can apply only to bodies; the souls are immortal and there is no question of their coming back to life.

It was not so for Daniel, who still believed in an early anthropology innocent of any Greek influence. Of course this anthropology did admit of a certain dualism in human nature, but this dualism was not that of Greek philosophy. In order to understand this, let us read again the account of the creation of human beings in Genesis 2:7.

> Then the Lord God formed man from the dust of the ground, and breathed into his nostrils the breath of life; and the man became a living being.

The first human being is essentially something fashioned by God from the clay of the earth. This being is so identified with this something drawn from the earth that the name of the first human, *ʾadam,* is derived from the Hebrew word that designates "ground" or "earth," *ʾadamah.* It is true that in order to become a "living being," the human needs an element not drawn from the earth, the vital breath which receives different names in the Bible: *neshama, nefesh,* or *ruah.* But whatever its name, this vital breath is simply a principle of biological life; it is never understood as a principle of knowledge, will, feelings. Human personality does not reside in this vital breath that God can withdraw at any time, when God deems it good. The human personality and consciousness are linked with what comes from the earth.

Hebrew anthropology–like popular Greek anthropology as it is still found in Homer–remains "primitive": it regards human beings in their psychosomatic unity.

> In Israelite thought man is conceived, not so much in dual fashion as 'body' and 'soul,' but synthetically as a unit of vital power or (in current terminology) a psycho-physical organism. This is to say, the various members and secretions of the body, such as the bones, the heart, the bowels, and the loins, as well as the flesh and the blood, can all be thought of as revealing psychical properties.[5]

In other words, the whole of human psychic life–knowledge, love, will, feelings–is an emanation of the human physical being. When the Bible speaks of God who "plumbs the depths of loins and hearts," we must take these words in their literal meaning: human psychic life comes from the human heart and loins, or, as the ancient Greeks would have said, from the human lungs and diaphragm. Thus, human personality resides neither in the human "soul," as Greek philosophy thought, nor in the "vital breath" communicated by God as a mere principle of biological life, but in the "earthy" being drawn from the earth.

And since, at death, the human heart, loins, and all other organs disappear in the earth, humans can no longer think, will, love, feel anything. They are no longer "living beings." From the human point of view, they are no longer anything but the shadows of themselves. A consequence of this for Daniel is that to rise again is to find again, not only a body, but the power to think, to will, to love. Obviously, this return to life necessarily entails God's "re-creating" in some way all the physical organs without which humans could not "live." This process of "resurrection" was well described by the prophet Ezekiel in the celebrated vision of the dry

---

[5] Johnson, *Vitality*, 87.

bones (ch. 37).[6] At the prophet's command, therefore at God's, the bones come together; then they are covered with sinews, the flesh comes back with all the organs necessary "to live," skin covers the whole body. Finally, the spirit, that is, the vital breath, returns and the people stand up on their feet: here they are, alive!

One can see the difference between this conception of the resurrection and what we hold nowadays: death is only a semblance since humans continue to live thanks to their immortal souls, the principle of psychic life. At the resurrection, all they do is find bodies again. For the Hebrews, on the contrary, humans lose almost every form of conscious life. At best, they are shades lost in darkness. But at the resurrection, they will again become beings of flesh and blood, able to think, to will, to feel. Without resurrection, human beings are but eternally recumbent statues, as cold, as motionless, and as dead as marble. By rising, they will be able to "live" again in the full sense of the word.

What Becomes of Human Beings at Death?

We have just said that for the Hebrews, in death, humans were at best shadows lost in darkness. Let us attempt to clarify this point.

a) According to a view frequently attested in the Bible, when they die, humans go down to Sheol. Situated under the earth, this dwelling of the dead closely resembles the Babylonian Arallu or the Hades of the early Greeks.[7] It is a region of complete darkness. The dead are there as "shades" (the Rephaim) with only a semblance of life. This absolute desolation of the sojourn of the dead is well described by the psalmist:

> For my soul is full of troubles,
> and my life draws near to Sheol.

[6] Here we have indeed the description of a resurrection, but it must be understood in the figurative and collective meaning: it is the people of God that comes back to life.

[7] See Dhorme, *Le séjour;* Tromp, *Primitive.*

> I am counted among those who go down to the Pit;
>   I am like those who have no help,
> like those forsaken among the dead,
>   like the slain that lie in the grave,
> like those whom you remember no more,
>   for they are cut off from your hand.
> You have put me in the depths of the Pit,
>   in the regions dark and deep.
>
>   . . . .
>
> Do you work wonders for the dead?
>   Do the shades rise up to praise you?
> Is your steadfast love declared in the grave,
>   or your faithfulness in Abaddon?
> Are your wonders known in the darkness,
>   or your saving help in the land of forgetfulness? (Ps 88:3-
>   6, 10-12).

In truth, the shades are not completely deprived of life; but they have kept only "the weakest form of life,"[8] perhaps because they still have their skeletons.

b) However, there is still a more radical way of conceiving the human state after death. It is based on the accounts in Genesis. Let us return to Genesis 2:7 concerning the creation of human beings and translate it most literally: "Then Yhwh God formed the human, dust [drawn] from the earth, [ʿaphar minhaʾadamah] and breathed into its nostrils a breath of life and the human became a living being." Therefore, the human being is mere "dust," and after the original sin, God can say to the man, in order to punish him for his fault, "By the sweat of your face you shall eat bread until you return to the ground, for out of it you were taken; you are dust, and to dust you shall return." There is no mention of Sheol in this text; there is something more basic here, the work of creation will be undone: the vital breath that God had given to humans will be withdrawn and they will return to the dust from which they were formed. Ecclesiastes says this very felicitously, "before . . . the dust returns to the earth as it was,

---

[8] Johnson, *Vitality*, 88.

and the breath returns to God who gave it" (12:7). In a still more dramatic manner, the same author, who did not believe in life after death, wrote:

> I said in my heart with regard to human beings that God is testing them to show that they are but animals. For the fate of humans and the fate of animals is the same; as one dies, so dies the other. They all have the same breath, and humans have no advantage over the animals; for all is vanity. All go to one place; all are from the dust, and all turn to dust again. Who knows whether the human spirit goes upward and the spirit of animals goes downward to the earth (Eccl 3:18-21)?[9]

This theme is found in other texts of the Bible:

> If [God] should take back his spirit to himself,
>   and gather to himself his breath,
> all flesh would perish together,
>   and all mortals return to dust (Job 34:14-15).[10]

> When you hide your face, they are dismayed;
>   when you take away their breath, they die
> and return to their dust (Ps 104:29).

> . . . these mortals who were made of earth a short time before
> and after a little while go to the earth from which all mortals
>   are taken,
> when the time comes to return the souls that were borrowed
>   (Wis 15:8).

In all these texts, the idea is very simple and, to repeat it once more, has its origin in Genesis 2:7 and 3:19: death is caused by God's taking back the vital breath God had "lent" humans; then, they return to the dust from which they were fashioned. There is no mention of any sort of descent into Sheol in these texts. After death, humans are nothing at all.

In what perspective does Daniel 12:2 find its place? In that of Genesis 2:7 and 3:19. Indeed, at the resurrection, there is no question of coming out of Sheol, but, for those who "are

---

[9] This last sentence, which is not in harmony with the previous context, seems to be an addition.

[10] See also Job 10:8-12, which is reminiscent of Gen 2:7.

sleeping in the Land of Dust," of awakening. We have followed the translation of the New Jerusalem Bible; however, let us make the translation even closer to the actual words. In Genesis 2:7, it is said that God formed the human [*ha'adam*], "dust [drawn] from the earth [*'aphar minha'adamah*]." This narrative wants to emphasize that the human, as its name indicates, is made of earth. In English, instead of calling the first human Adam, it would be better to call it "Earth Creature." In this case, the text of Genesis would become, "God formed the Earth Creature, dust coming from earth." Let us come back to the text of Daniel 12:2; it speaks of those who sleep "in the Land of Dust" (*'admat 'aphar*). We have seen that here Daniel repeats Isaiah 26:19 which mentions the "dwellers in the dust." But if Daniel completes the text, it is certainly in order to refer to Genesis 2:7 with its coupling of "Earth Creature" (Adam) and "dust [drawn] from the earth." For Daniel, at death, humans do not go down to Sheol, but, being "taken from the earth," they simply return to the earth from which they were taken (see Gen 3:19). Lying in their tombs, humans seem to "sleep" while waiting for the day when they "will awaken." What we call "resurrection" is seen as an awakening. We shall find these expressions again in numerous texts of the New Testament.

Those Who Will Rise

But we are not at the end of our difficulties with the text of Daniel 12:2. We have quoted it according to the translation of the New Jerusalem Bible, "Of those who are sleeping in the Land of Dust, many will awaken, some to everlasting life, some to everlasting [horror]." A difficulty is immediately apparent. According to this translation, the resurrection of the dead would not be general since it would concern only "many" among the dead. What would be the criterion of distinction? It is impossible to know. The first thought that comes to mind would be a distinction between the righteous and the evildoers, but this is not the case since a certain number of those who arise are destined for "eternal horror." Therefore, the resurrection would concern only some of the righteous and some of the evildoers. But why? One can doubt that Daniel conceived of a resurrection of the wicked. We have seen that he repeats various texts from Isaiah, especially 26:19. Now, Isaiah 26:19 speaks only of the righteous. About the wicked, he says on the contrary, "The dead do not live; / shades do not rise— / because you have punished and destroyed them, / and wiped out all memory of them" (26:14).

Bernard Alfrink[11] clearly saw this difficulty and, in order to avoid it, proposed a new interpretation of the text of Daniel 12:2. The words, "some . . . some" are the translation the New Jerusalem Bible adopted for the Hebrew expression *'elleh . . . we'elleh*. In the Bible, this is used in two ways. One is to distinguish two parts in one group which was just mentioned; this is the meaning chosen by the New Jerusalem Bible. In the other, the expression can apply to two groups which were distinguished in a previous context. Let us see whether this second sense could be apposite here.

At the end of chapter 11, Daniel describes an invasion which will ravage "the Land of Splendour," Palestine (11:41; NJB). The invaders will establish their headquarters "between the sea and the mountain of the Holy Splendour" (11:45; NJB), in the whole region that lies east of the Mediterranean. Many will be put to death (11:41) and this "will be a time of great distress, unparalleled since nations came into existence" (12:1a; NJB). Fortunately, Michael, the angel who protects God's people, will come to their help so that "your own people will be spared—all those whose names are found written in the Book" (12:1b; NJB). Among all those still alive at the time of the great eschatological trial, there will be a separation: some will be put to death by the invaders; others, those who are listed in the book of life, will escape the massacre. In 12:2a, Daniel examines the fate of those who had died before the devastating invasion. A distinction will be made among those also since only "many"

---

[11] Alfrink, *L'idée*. Many commentators have adopted Alfrink's position. See the list of them in Puech, *La Croyance*, 80; he himself has endorsed it.

who are sleeping in the land of dust will awaken. The others will not wake but will remain in death.

If we bring the two perspectives together, we have two distinct groups: on the one hand, all those destined for death, whether they were killed at the time of the invasion or do not rise. On the other hand, all those destined for life, whether they escaped being destroyed at the time of the final invasion or awaken from their sleep of death. These are the two groups spoken of in verse 12b, not to be grammatically linked with verse 12a, but forming a separate sentence with the verb "to be" understood, as is often the case in biblical Hebrew. So, verse 12b should be translated, "these [are] for everlasting life, those [are] for everlasting horror." The demonstrative pronoun "these" designates both those who have escaped the great invasion and those who have risen; the demonstrative pronoun "those" designates both the victims of the great invasion and those who will not rise but will remain in death. Although Daniel does not explicitly say it, only the righteous will awaken from the sleep of death. God's new people will comprise the survivors of the great invasion and those who will rise from death. The others will fall prey to "everlasting horror." Interpreted in this way, Daniel's text does not stumble into the difficulties mentioned above.[12]

The New World

How does Daniel visualize the world in which God's new people—those who escaped destruction at the time of the great eschatological trial and those who have risen from the sleep of death—are going to live once their enemies are reduced to powerlessness?

The events of which Daniel speaks take place "at the time of the End" (11:40; 12:9; NJB), "at that time" (12:1;

[12] As an objection to this interpretation of Daniel, one can put forward the text of John 5:28-29, which seems to interpret Dan 12:2 according to the translation of the NJB. But it is not certain that John is quoting Dan 12:2; the expression "those who are in their graves" seems rather to recall LXX Isa 26:19.

NJB), "at the end of time" (12:13; NJB). When reading these expressions, many could be tempted to give them the cosmic sense to which we are accustomed when we speak of "the end of the world." Daniel would already have thought of the destruction of the material world in which we now live, making room for another world with changed physical conditions. But this would be attributing to Daniel ideas he did not have. The expression "at the end of time" (12:13) must be understood in relation to verses 11-12, in which it is said that the persecution by Antiochus Epiphanes and the reign of evil must last for either 1290 days or 1335 days. What is meant is the end of the days during which the tyrant will persecute God's people. As a consequence, "the time of the End" spoken of in 11:40 and 12:9 designates the time when the persecution against God's people will come to an end (see 11:27, 45; 12:7). This end is not that of the physical world in which we live, but of a period of upheaval and persecution. God's people will be able to live in peace because their persecutors will have disappeared from the earth.

However, Daniel writes in 12:3, "Those who are wise will shine as brightly as the expanse of the heavens, and those who have instructed many in uprightness [cf. Isa 53:11], as bright as stars for all eternity" (NJB). A note to this verse in the Bible de Jérusalem explains, "The preceding verse suggests that the reference here is not only to the great name that the devout leave behind them, as in Wisdom 3:7 (cf. Isa 1:31), but to an eschatological transformation of the whole person into a glorified state." However, if Daniel had wanted to give in 12:3 a description of what the risen will be like physically, why would he speak only of the "wise" (see 11:33, 35; 12:10), of "those who have instructed many in uprightness"?[13] The following reflections agree with the direction suggested by Pierre Grelot:[14]

> The hypothesis of a speculation on astral immortality is out of the question. One can even wonder whether the text alludes

---

[13] The two expressions are equivalent. See Puech, *La Croyance*, 82.
[14] Grelot, *Histoire*, 96.

> to the general metamorphosis of the elect in a transfigured universe or, through this image, to the proper role of the 'wise'–those who have withstood the trial even to the point of death and those who will continue to play the same role among the saved people.

This latter alternative is the one to choose.

Indeed, by mentioning those who will have taught others to live according to God's will, Daniel here is speaking of morality. The text of Daniel 12:3 must be interpreted from an ethical point of view; and many texts, biblical or otherwise, prompt us to do so. In the Bible, the word of God is often compared to a lamp, to a light that illuminates the way leading to God, to life (for instance, Ps 119:105; Prov 6:23). This is expressed even more clearly in the apocryphal book of Enoch, "Then shall wisdom be given to the elect, and all of them shall live and shall sin no more. . . . In an intelligent man it [wisdom] is illumination, and to a prudent man it is understanding" (5:8). Here, it is wisdom which is compared to a light enabling humans not to sin any more. People themselves can be likened to stars inasmuch as their good behavior enlightens others concerning the way one must live in order to please God. In a fragment of the Testament of Levi (Greek 14:3-4) discovered in Qumran, one reads, "The sun, the moon, and the stars . . . [shine above the earth. Do you not resemble the sun and] the moon? If you become obscured [through impiety, what will] the nations [do]?"[15] Similarly, Jesus will tell his disciples, "You are the light of the world. . . . Let your light shine before others, so that they may see your good works and give glory to your Father in heaven" (Matt 5:14, 16). Daniel 12:3 must be interpreted in reference to all these texts. In the eschatological world, inhabited by survivors of the great devastating invasion and those who have risen, the "wise" will shine like stars in the sense that they will teach people how to live in accordance with the divine decree and that they will be listened to by all and will be perfectly obeyed. Only the righteous will form

---

[15] Quoted by Milik, *Problèmes*, 345.

the new people of God (cf. Isa 60:21). There is no question here of a physical transformation of the risen.

Therefore, nothing allows us to think Daniel envisaged that the chosen people's destiny would not be realized on earth, albeit an idealized earth. Since, as we have seen above, the resurrection of the dead will mark the end of the curse that burdened humanity according to Genesis 3:19, there will not be any death. In the last analysis, we agree with Grelot's words following those quoted above:

> If we except an insistence on individual retribution, insured by the resurrection of the righteous put to death (12:2), is this conception of the 'world to come' very different from that found in a text such as Zechariah 14:6-11, 16-21? Nevertheless, the expression 'everlasting life' appears to allude to a definitive triumph of God over death; here, one comes very near to the vista opened by Isaiah 25:6-8.

In chapter 14, Zechariah saw the destiny of God's people as being realized on earth.

In summary, here is how we can visualize the events of the "time of the End" of which Daniel speaks. God's people will have to contend with a period of violent persecution and distress beyond words (11:41a; 12:2b). But God, through the intermediary of the angel Michael, will intervene to bring this somber period to an end (12:1). At that time, all the righteous will rise from their sleep of death (12:2). They are no longer anything but "dust"; however, they will come back to life as if by a re-creation of their physical elements. Joining those who will have escaped the great eschatological trial, they will form the new people of God on an earth whose physical conditions will have changed, especially in that death will have been abolished. Humanity will recover in a sort of regained "earthly paradise" the state it had before the original sin. The members of this people will be morally transformed, perfectly submissive to God's will. Then an era of peace, joy, and light will begin.

2

The Second Book of Maccabees

The second book of Maccabees is an abridgement of a work in five volumes written by a certain Jason of Cyrene (2 Macc 2:23-32), about whom we know nothing beyond his name. That work was a narrative of the events that occurred under the reign of Antiochus Epiphanes, the persecutor of those Jews who wanted to remain faithful to the divine law. Jason wrote it shortly after the events, about 160–150 B.C.E., which brings us to a period slightly more recent than Daniel's oracles. In 124 B.C.E., the anonymous compiler, who wrote in Greek, composed the work we now possess.[16]

Faith in Resurrection

Seven brothers have been arrested with their mother, and King Antiochus wants to force them to eat pork, a food prohibited by the Law. To succeed in his endeavor, he subjects the brothers to torture in their mother's presence, one after the other (7:1). Before being tortured, each one of the seven brothers has time to address a speech to the tyrant in which each expresses his eagerness to die for God and God's laws. Two among them take this occasion to affirm their faith in the resurrection. Thus the second brother flings these words into

---

[16] For additional details, see Puech, *La Croyance*, 85.

the king's face, "You accursed wretch, you dismiss us from this present life, but the King of the universe will raise us up to an everlasting renewal of life" (7:9). In his turn, the fourth brother proclaims, "One cannot but choose to die at the hands of mortals and cherish the hope God gives of being raised again by him" (7:14). Finally, to encourage her sons, the valiant mother says, "Therefore the Creator of the world . . . will in his mercy give life and breath back to you again, since you now forget yourselves for the sake of his laws" (7:23).

As we have seen concerning Daniel, a Jew could not conceive of a return to life without a sort of re-creation by God of all the physical elements that compose human beings. Likewise, Razis, one of the elders of Jerusalem, about to die for his faith, throws himself from the height of a wall. "With his blood now completely drained from him, he tore out his entrails, took them in both hands and hurled them at the crowd, calling upon the Lord of life and spirit to give them back to him again. This was the manner of his death" (14:46).

The Resurrection Reserved for the Righteous Alone

For Jason of Cyrene as for Daniel, the resurrection is exclusively for the righteous. The fourth brother asserts it when he says to Antiochus, "For you there will be no resurrection to life" (7:14). Some commentators have interpreted this passage in the sense that by depriving the tyrant of a "resurrection to life," the fourth brother was implicitly promising him a "resurrection to death" (cf. John 5:28-29). But if such had been the author's thought, he would have explicitly said so, rather than speak in this ambiguous way. In any event, we have another text in which we clearly see that for Jason, the wicked must not have the benefit of a future resurrection. During a battle, a certain number of Jews are killed by the enemy. At the time of burial, it is discovered that they wore on their persons "sacred tokens of the idols of Jamnia," something prohibited by the Law; their deaths are seen as a punishment inflicted by God (12:38-42). Consequently, Judas Maccabeus orders a sacrifice for those who have died under such circumstances:

He also took up a collection, man by man, to the amount of two thousand drachmas of silver, and sent it to Jerusalem to provide for a sin offering. In doing this he acted very well and honorably, taking account of the resurrection. For if he were not expecting that those who had fallen would rise again, it would have been superfluous and foolish to pray for the dead. But if he was looking to the splendid reward that is laid up for those who fall asleep in godliness, it was a holy and pious thought. Therefore he made atonement for the dead, so that they might be delivered from their sin (12:43-45).

Judas believes in the resurrection, but he thinks that those who die in a state of sin, in rebellion against the Law, cannot rise from the dead. Therefore, he has a sacrifice offered to expiate the sin of those who hid stolen tokens on their persons. From all this, it is clear that the resurrection is reserved solely for the "righteous" or perhaps those who, having died in a state of sin, have been made "righteous" through an expiatory sacrifice offered after their death.

The Time of the Resurrection

The resurrection of the dead will take place in the future, at a time not specified by the author. However, by bringing together some passages of the book, it is possible to relate this event to the restoration of God's people, as in Daniel's prophecies. In 7:29, the mother says to her youngest son, "Do not fear this butcher, but prove worthy of your brothers. Accept death, so that in God's mercy I may get you back again along with your brothers" (NJB). Obviously, it is thanks to the resurrection that the mother and her seven sons will be reunited. Now, this event will occur "in the day of mercy," which must be understood as that day when God will show mercy to God's people by granting a complete and definitive victory over all their enemies (cf. 8:5, 27; 11:10). It is therefore when God will effect the decisive restoration of God's people that the righteous will be raised so that they may share in the destiny of the new people. The perspective is the same as that of Daniel's oracles.

The Soul and the Body

One problem remains to be solved. How did Jason of Cyrene understand the resurrection? Was he still faithful to the Semitic anthropology which looked at humans in their psychosomatic unity? Or in accord with Greek philosophy, did he distinguish in human nature the soul and the body? If this was the case, did he follow Plato in his belief that the soul is immortal by nature, which would imply that for him, the resurrection concerned only the body?

Twice, the author of 2 Maccabees recognizes in humans two components that seem to be the soul and the body. He attributes the following words to Eleazar, this teacher of the Law whose martyrdom took place before that of the seven brothers and their mother:

> It is clear to the LORD in his holy knowledge that, though I might have been saved from death, I am enduring terrible sufferings in my body under this beating, but in my soul I am glad to suffer these things because I fear him (6:30).

In another passage, the emotion of the high priest, about to witness the profanation of the Temple, is described in these terms:

> To see the appearance of the high priest was to be wounded at heart, for his face and the change in his color disclosed the anguish of his soul. For terror and bodily trembling had come over the man, which plainly showed to those who looked at him the pain lodged in his heart (3:16-17).

The body is the part of humans which one sees and touches, the part which undergoes suffering. Another passage confirms this. The question is put to one of the brothers, "Will you eat rather than have your body punished limb by limb?" (7:7; cf. 9:7). The soul, for its part, is the principle of our passions and feelings. Antiochus is furious "in his soul." Faced with the assurance of one of the seven brothers, he cannot help but admire the young man's "soul"; it is the soul which is the source of his courage before the pain about to be inflicted on his body (7:12). Bravery in battle comes from the soul, as does the valor which transforms the young into mature men (15:17). This way of speaking, foreign to Hebrew thought, is influenced by the language of Greek philosophy. But it is Stoic philosophy. The author of 2 Maccabees does not accept that the soul is immortal by nature as did Plato. At death, it perishes along with the body. The youngest of the seven brothers acknowledges it, "I, like my brothers, give up body and life for the laws of our ancestors" (7:37; cf. 14:38).

What is effected at the resurrection is not the reunion of an immortal soul with its body, but the return of both soul and body to life.

Indeed, the soul is not immortal because it is not the principle of life. For the soul and body to "live," God must bestow on them the "breath of life" spoken of in Genesis 2:7. It is to this text that the mother of the seven brothers alludes when she says, "It was not I who gave you life and breath. . . . Therefore the Creator of the world, who shaped the beginning of humankind . . . will in his mercy give life and breath back to you again" (7:22-23). Life is linked, not with the soul, but with the vital breath that God grants to humans, takes back at the moment of death (3:31; 7:9a), and will give back at the resurrection (14:46).

Even though he adopted some ideas from Stoicism, the author of 2 Maccabees sees the resurrection as did Daniel: at death, humans sink into sleep (12:45) from which they will awaken only on the day of the resurrection. Let us add that he never envisages a physical transformation of the world to come: after the resurrection, God's new people will continue to live on earth, but in peace because their enemies will have been punished by God.

3

The First Letter of Paul to the Thessalonians

—— (4:13-18) ——

In the course of his second missionary journey, Paul evangelized the city of Thessalonica and established there a Christian community (Acts 17:1-9). Afterwards, he went to Athens (17:15-34), then to Corinth (18:1-17), where he learned that the new converts of Thessalonica were being persecuted by the pagans (1 Thess 2:14). Unable to come in person to comfort them (2:18), he sent them a letter through his disciple Timothy (3:2-3). This letter is 1 Thessalonians.

The Parousia[17]

From the beginning of his letter (1:9-10), Paul reminds the Christians of Thessalonica of the essential points of his preaching: to turn to the living God by abandoning idols; to wait for God's Son, who was raised from the dead, who is to come back from heaven to save us from the divine wrath. Therefore, the Christians are to live in the expectation of Christ's return, which can happen any moment.

---

[17] This word, transcribed from the Greek, designates the return of Christ. Later on in this book, we will give a fuller explanation of its meaning (see pp. 26–27).

At this time, the theme of the parousia holds a place of primordial importance in Paul's preoccupations: four times in the remainder of his letter, he comes back to Christ's "coming" (2:19; 3:13; 4:15; 5:23), which he calls Christ's parousia. This parousia will signal the beginning of God's reign (2:12). But for us to have a part in this reign, it is necessary that at his return Christ finds our "hearts strengthened in holiness" and us "blameless before our God" (see 3:13; cf. 5:23), living according to the moral prescriptions which Paul describes in 4:3-8. Otherwise, divine wrath would fall upon us (1:10).

It is obvious that Paul expects this parousia in the near future. He himself hopes to still be alive when this event takes place (4:15-17), and the Christians to whom he addresses his letter must live in all holiness so as to be found with pure hearts when Christ returns (3:13).

The Resurrection of the Dead

However, because some members of the community had died since Paul had left them, the Christians of Thessalonica must have been faced with a crucial problem. Or, more simply, being subjected to persecution, they might have feared being put to death before the parousia. In either case, they must have wondered how the dead could have a part in the reign which Christ was to inaugurate at his return. And Paul was probably so convinced of the imminence of the parousia that he had not thought it necessary to discuss this problem with the community. Now he does so in his letter (4:13-18):

> 13. But we do not want you to be uninformed, brothers and sisters, about those who have died, so that you may not grieve as others do who have no hope.
> 14. For since we believe that Jesus died and rose again, even so, through Jesus, God will bring with him those who have died.
> 15. For this we declare to you by the word of the Lord, that we who are alive, who are left until the coming of the Lord, will by no means precede those who have died.

16. For the Lord himself, with a cry of command, with the archangel's call and with the sound of God's trumpet, will descend from heaven, and the dead in Christ will rise first.
17. Then we who are alive, who are left, will be caught up in the clouds together with them to meet the Lord in the air, and so we will be with the Lord forever.
18. Therefore encourage one another with these words.

Thus, at the parousia, those who "fell asleep in Jesus" (NJB) will rise and join the living to go and meet Christ. They will in no way be put at a disadvantage in relation to those who will still be alive at that time.

But how does Paul visualize this resurrection? Does he think of an immortal soul that would simply find its body again? Absolutely not. Paul remains in the tradition inherited from Daniel: it is the whole human being who disappears in death and will come back to life. His language confirms this. "Those who have died" will rise, and not merely their bodies (4:16). The dead are said to have "fallen asleep" (4:13, 14, 15; NJB), an expression borrowed from Daniel and out of place if, at that point in his life,[18] Paul accepted an immortal soul already dwelling with God. Finally, if Paul and the faithful of Thessalonica believed that those who to all appearances have died are in reality alive in God through their immortal souls, what problem would Christ's parousia pose? No, Paul's position is similar to Daniel's: if it happens that some Christians "fall asleep," body and soul, before the parousia, they will stand up again, they will rise, body and soul, when Christ returns to initiate God's reign. Similarly as in Daniel, they will, together with the group of those still alive, form God's new people.

Some will object that in 5:23, Paul seems to distinguish three components in human nature: spirit, soul, and body. Much discussion has centered on this passage. A hypothesis proposed by some commentators is that here Paul names certain aspects of the human being without really distinguishing

---

[18] In 2 Cor and subsequently, Paul will adopt positions that will show him closer to Platonic philosophy.

spirit, soul, and body. This is possible, but it is preferable to observe that even if Paul accepted a real distinction between the body and the soul, nothing would allow us to think that he would have adopted the Platonic idea of a soul immortal by nature. Like the followers of Stoic philosophy, he could have distinguished the soul and the body without at the same time believing that the soul is immortal. This was, we have seen, the position of the author of 2 Maccabees.

The Reign of God

There remains one problem to solve. The parousia of Christ marks the beginning of the reign of God (2:12). But how does Paul see this reign? Is it a purely celestial reign, in God, or, as Daniel thought, a reign to be established on earth? This latter hypothesis seems the more plausible for the following reasons:[19]

Paul uses the term *parousia* to signify Christ's return. This noun, very rare in the Septuagint (Jdt; 2 and 3 Macc), has no equivalent in biblical Hebrew. Of course, the idea that God is to "come" is frequent in the Old Testament, but it is always expressed by means of a verb, not a noun. On the other hand, "parousia" was a quasi-technical term to designate the arrival of a king or an emperor in a city belonging to him, when this visit was a somewhat formal occasion.

For his part, Paul writes that at Christ's parousia, those who are still alive and those who have just risen from the dead will be taken into the air "to meet the Lord." Here again, Paul uses a quasi-technical expression designating the ceremonial of the king's solemn entry into one of his cities. Carrying flowers, crowns, foliage, the people set out "to meet" the sovereign at a certain distance from the city. All came back to the city escorting the king as a mark of honor.[20] This is the scenario described for instance in John 12:12-15, the solemn entry of Jesus into Jerusalem when he was acclaimed "king of Israel."

---

[19] For what follows, see Deissmann, *Licht*, 314–320; Guntermann, *Die Eschatologie*, 29; Dupont *ΣΥΝ ΧΡΙΣΤΩΙ*, 49ff.

[20] See Josephus, *Ant.* 11.8.4; *War* 7.100–103.

Lastly, it is worth noting Paul's insistence in this whole passage on giving Christ his royal title of "Lord" (4:15, 16, 17a, 17b).

Here is, therefore, how we must understand this passage in Paul's letter: in a relatively near future, Christ will come down from heaven (where he has been residing since his resurrection) in order to make his solemn entrance, his parousia, into the city of which he is the "Lord." At that time, the Christians who are already dead will rise, and all, those who still are alive and those who have just risen from the dead, will be carried "in the air" to meet him, not to go with him into heaven, but to return with him to earth as a solemn escort.

In 1 Thessalonians, Paul retains Daniel's perspective: the eschatological reign will be established on earth.[21] Is this not what the disciples had in mind when they asked on the day Jesus ascended into heaven, "Lord, is this the time when you will restore the kingdom to Israel?" (Acts 1:6)? Without a doubt, the earth will be transformed by the divine glory (1 Thess 2:12) since the believers will be able to be lifted into the air to meet their Lord. Paul admits this implicitly in the present passage, and he will affirm it explicitly in 1 Corinthians 15:50-55 (cf. Rom 8:19-22). Still, it remains that the reign of God will have the earth for its theater. However, it will not be long before Paul abandons this idea, as we shall see when we analyze the text of 1 Corinthians. We shall then observe how his thought evolved on this precise point.

The Fate of the Impious

Paul does not explicitly speak of the fate of the sinners who will have died before the parousia. However, it is clear that the entire scenario described in 4:13-18 concerns only those who have fallen asleep in the Lord. Did he envisage a resurrection for the impious? It is quite improbable. For

---

[21] This fact will be confirmed in the following chapter: by analyzing 1 Cor 15:16-28 (pp. 29–34), we shall see that Paul conceived of an intermediate reign here on earth between the parousia and the end of time.

Paul as for Daniel, they will not rise; they will remain in the state of "the dead."[22]

As for the impious who will still be alive at the parousia, they will be the object of God's wrath (1:10), they will be doomed to destruction (5:3). Paul does not make clear in what this destruction will consist. But the whole development of 5:1-3 offers analogies with what Luke writes in 21:34-35. The catastrophe will swallow up "all who live on the face of the whole earth." This last expression is reminiscent of Genesis 7:23, which speaks of the flood. In Luke 17:26-27, there is another allusion to the flood which will submerge the wicked at the time the Son of Man returns. One is led to think that perhaps Paul had in mind a disaster similar to the flood or the destruction of Sodom (see Luke 17:28-30). This catastrophe will cause the ruin of evildoers, whereas those faithful to Christ will be saved by him (1:10).

---

[22] Let us make clear here that Paul *does not teach* that sinners will not rise; we can only conjecture that when he wrote 1 Thessalonians, he did not envisage such a resurrection.

—— 4 ——

The First Letter of Paul to the Corinthians

—— (15:22-28) ——

In order to illustrate what we were just saying concerning Paul's belief in an earthly reign to be inaugurated by Christ's parousia, let us without delay analyze the text of 1 Corinthians 15:22-28, the last one in which Paul still speaks of the parousia.[23]

There was a time when many exegetes held that 1 Corinthians was composed of different fragments, a hypothesis now abandoned. However, we are going to see that perhaps it should be rehabilitated, at least as far as 15:16-28 is concerned. Paul himself informs us (1 Cor 5:9-13) that he already had written a letter to the faithful of Corinth, a letter now lost. If the analysis that we are going to propose is accepted, it will be easy to imagine that the little fragment which we are singling out is part of the letter Paul alludes to.

A Doublet in 1 Corinthians 15:16-28

1 Corinthians 15:16-28 contains several verses which are a doublet of other verses in chapter 15.

---

[23] The ideas we are about to present in this chapter are, as far as we know, relatively new.

15:13-14	*15:16-17*
If there is no resurrection of the dead, then Christ has not been raised, and if Christ has not been raised then our proclamation has been in vain and your faith has been in vain.	For if the dead are not raised, then Christ has not been raised. If Christ has not been raised, your faith is futile.

The doublet is obvious, and it is difficult to believe that Paul would have thus copied himself in the course of the same letter.

But this doublet is part of two parallel texts that are more complete. Let us observe that verses 20-28 address the problem of the resurrection of the dead, as do verses 35-55 (albeit in a much more thorough way). The first of these two developments (vv. 20-28) ends with the affirmation that death is destroyed (v. 26); the same is true of the second text (vv. 54-55). Now, as we shall see in more detail later, these two developments are incompatible: in the first, resurrection of the dead and definitive destruction of death do not happen at the same time, whereas they are simultaneous in the second. Lastly, let us note that verse 35, which raises the question, "But someone will ask, 'How are the dead raised?'" seems to follow logically the end of verse 15, "if it is true that the dead are not raised."

In view of all this, here is the solution we propose. We are faced with two parallel developments belonging to two different letters. The first development, the earlier as we shall see, contained verses 16-28 (plus possibly some minor glosses that are not worth going into). The second development contained verses 12-15 and continued with verses 35-56.

An Intermediate Reign

Here is the text of 1 Corinthians 15:22-28,[24] arranged on the basis of the analysis done by J. Lambrecht.[25] Paul begins

[24] Among Paul's letters this passage is one of the most debated.
[25] Lambrecht, "Structure."

by enunciating his thesis, in verses 23-24; then he supplies explanations of his thesis in verses 25-28a; verse 28b returns—forming an inclusion—to the idea of verse 24:

> 22. For as all die in Adam, so all will be made alive in Christ.
> 23. But each in his own order: Christ the first fruits, then at his coming those who belong to Christ.
> 24. Then comes the end, when he hands over the kingdom to God the Father, after he has destroyed every ruler and every authority and power.
>   25. For he must reign until he has put all his enemies under his feet.
> 26. The last enemy to be destroyed is death.
> 27. For God has placed all things in subjection under his feet. . . .
> 28. When all things are subjected to him, then the Son himself will also be subjected to the one who put all things in subjection under him, so that God may be all in all.

a) In this text, Paul underlines three successive phases. First, the resurrection of Christ. Second, the resurrection of those who belong to Christ, at the time of the parousia. Third, the end,[26] when Christ will hand over the rule to God. In verse 25, Paul explains what will happen at the parousia: Christ will come back to reign until he has defeated all his enemies. Where is this reign of Christ going to take place? Paul does not say explicitly, but the term parousia suggests that it will be on earth, as we have explained when speaking of 1 Thessalonians 4:13-18. We then understand that the reign of Christ (v. 25) can be distinguished from the reign of God (v. 28). Besides, the resurrection of the dead does not coincide with the definitive destruction of death. This will happen only at the end of Christ's reign; during this reign, Christ will overcome all his enemies, and

---

[26] With Lambrecht and many others, we translate *to telos* by "the end," not by "the rest"; we shall see later that this translation is supported by the parallel text from Revelation which we shall quote on pp. 32–34. We therefore part company with those who have wanted to see here an allusion to a second group of risen people.

death will be abolished last of all. The perspective is different from what it is in 1 Corinthians 15:51-54, where resurrection of the dead and definitive victory over death are to happen together at the return of Christ. Here, on the contrary, the resurrection of the dead is placed at the beginning of the earthly reign of Christ, at the parousia, and the victory over death at the end of this reign.

Therefore, this is the scenario Paul has in mind. First phase, the resurrection of Christ. Second phase, the resurrection of those who belong to Christ, which coincides with the parousia. Paul explains that this coming of Christ will mark the beginning of his reign (on earth) during which he will reduce all his enemies to powerlessness. Third phase, "the end," when the last enemy, death, will have been vanquished and Christ will place the kingdom in his Father's hands.

b) This exegesis is confirmed by a comparison between this passage in Paul's letter and what we read in Revelation 19–21. In this text, we find the same scheme as in Paul's letter, only more fully developed.

– In 19:11-13, there is the return of Christ to earth. He arrives as "King of kings and Lord of lords" (19:16).

– He goes into war in order to exterminate his people's enemies: the beast, the kings of the earth in league with the beast, the false prophet; all are thrown into the lake of fire or given as food to the vultures (19:17-21).

This victory of Christ the king is completed by the coming of an angel who throws the dragon, that is, the devil, into the bottomless pit, where he will remain as long as Christ's reign on earth lasts, one thousand years.

– Then comes the mention of the martyrs' resurrection (20:4). It is not explicitly said that this resurrection will occur at the time of Christ's return (as in Paul); however, the two events are linked since these risen martyrs will reign with Christ for one thousand years, that is, for the duration assigned to his reign on earth.

– There follows an episode that has no counterpart in Paul: when the thousand years are ended, Satan will be released from his prison; he will come and ravage the land

(Palestine) and lay siege to the beloved city (Jerusalem). But he will be overcome and thrown into the lake of fire where he will rejoin the beast and the false prophet (Rev 20:7-10).

We must note one important detail: verse 7 begins with the expression "when the thousand years are ended" [*hotan telesthē*], that is, when the reign of Christ comes to an end. One sees the closeness of this expression to the "then comes the end" [*eita to telos*], which in Paul marks the end of Christ's reign (1 Cor 15:24a).

– Then comes the resurrection of the dead (20:11-13).

– Finally, Death and Hades are thrown into the lake of fire, as had been the beast and then Satan. As in Paul, it is the last enemy to be conquered.

– At last, the universe is transformed (21:1-2) and God comes to dwell with humankind: "He will dwell with them as their God; / they will be his peoples, / and God himself will be with them" (21:3). The seer returns to the idea that death has no place in the new world (21:4). It is God's reign which succeeds Christ's, as for Paul in 1 Corinthians 15:24, 28, the latter verse stating that "God [will] be all in all."

Readers will have noticed that two events are split in two in Revelation, because of the splitting of the characters involved into two groups: those at the time of the destruction of the enemies and those at the resurrection. The beast and its satellites are the first to be destroyed (19:11-21), then Satan (20:7b-10). The martyrs are the first to be raised (20:4), then other human beings (20:11-13). If we eliminate one of the terms of the doublets, we arrive at a scheme quasi-identical with Paul's, even though the events are not cited in the same order. The return of Christ, who comes to reign on earth, will be concomitant with the resurrection of the dead (or the martyrs). During his reign, Christ will exterminate all the enemies of his people. At the close of his reign *(eita to telos/ hotan telesthē),* the last enemy, death, will be destroyed. At that moment, God's reign will succeed Christ's.

Did the author of Revelation rely on Paul? It seems more probable to us that both Paul and the author of Revelation followed a common scenario which they found in the early Christian tradition. Paul delivers it to us almost in its original form, just as he offers us in 15:3-7 a fragment of the apostolic preaching. In contrast, the author of Revelation gives free rein to imagination in order to develop this scheme into a series of impressive scenes.

c) Let us draw an important conclusion from these explanations. In Revelation, it is clear that this "intermediate" reign of Christ takes place on earth, as is shown by the description of the great eschatological trial resulting in the invasion of the land and the siege of Jerusalem, the beloved city (20:9). Similarly, Paul places the reign of Christ on earth since the word "parousia" suggests the entrance of the king into his city, as we have said concerning 1 Thessalonians 4:13-18. The conclusions deduced from our exposition of this text from 1 Thessalonians are thereby confirmed. But since then, Paul's thought has evolved. In 1 Thessalonians, he did not envision any end to the earthly reign of Christ. Here, he sees a term to it: it will be replaced by God's reign, probably in heaven. We shall see further in the next chapter that Paul will abandon this idea of an earthly reign of Christ because resurrection of the dead and transformation into a glorious state for all people must happen at the same moment, at Christ's return (see 1 Cor 15:51-54).

— 5 —

The First Letter of Paul to the Corinthians

— (15:35-57) —

Paul wrote 1 Corinthians around Easter 57. The fundamental text—15:35-57—presents many difficulties and has given rise to erroneous ideas concerning Paul's teaching on the resurrection.

The Problem of the "Body"

Before analyzing Paul's text in detail, it is important to be clear on a point that commands the interpretation of the whole passage.

In verse 35, Paul enunciates the question he is going to answer, "But someone will ask, 'How are the dead raised? With what kind of body do they come?'" In verse 44, he explains that if one sows a "psychic" [literally translated from Greek *psuchikon*][27] body, it is a spiritual body that is raised. Paul might appear to accept a distinction between the body and the soul as in Greek philosophy. During this life, the body is animated by the *psuchē*, the soul, whereas after the resurrection, it will be vivified by the spirit. Here he seems to believe that the soul is immortal, if not by nature, at least in

---

[27] Animated by the *psuchē*, the soul.

virtue of a privilege granted by God. The resurrection would consist in the soul's rejoining a body, which will happen at the time of Christ's return, as he will say later. Paul would then have adopted the position which is currently taught today. But let us have a closer look at the texts.

a) It is true that if the Greek word *sōma* can mean the human body as opposed to the soul, this meaning is only secondary and derives from philosophical reflection. In common parlance, the word has a far less precise meaning. One can become convinced of this simply by consulting the Liddell-Scott Greek-English dictionary. In Homer, the word meant "dead body, corpse." Later on, it came to mean "animated body, either human or animal." Thus the expression *to son sōma* can be translated "your person," that is, "you." Similarly, the phrase *doula kai eleuthera sōmata* means "human beings, either slaves or free." Let us add one example from 2 Maccabees 12:26, where it is said that Judas Maccabeus ordered the slaughter of twenty-five thousand *sōmata*, that is, twenty-five thousand people. No need to pursue this further; it is sufficient to remember the very vague meaning of "being" which seems to have been quite current.[28]

Let us see how Paul uses the term in our passage, elsewhere than in the two verses quoted above (vv. 35 and 44). To explain with what *sōma* humans will rise, he begins (vv. 37-38) by giving a comparison taken from ordinary rural life: "And as for what you sow, you do not sow the body that is to be, but a bare seed, perhaps of wheat or some other grain. But God gives it a body [*sōma*] as he has chosen, and to each kind of seed its own body [*sōma*]." What will sprout after the sowing is a plant made up of stalk and leaves. It is obvious that here the word does not have the meaning of "body" as opposed to the soul, but should be translated by "being." In verses 40-41, still explaining the resurrection, Paul gives another comparison based on the opposition existing between the earthly *sōmata* and the heavenly *sōmata*. The first comprise human beings, cattle, birds, and fish (v. 39); the second, sun, moon,

---

[28] But a "being" inasmuch as it is made of physical elements.

and stars (v. 41). It is clear that here, too, the plural *sōmata* does not mean "bodies," but should be rendered by "beings" as in the previous example. There are heavenly beings and earthly beings. One conclusion necessarily follows. If Paul gives the word *sōma* the meaning of "being," not "body" (distinct from the soul) in the two examples he presents to explain how the resurrection happens, then the same must certainly be said of verse 35, and also of verse 44, as we shall see later on.

b) Other clues enable us to suppose that in this passage, Paul does not think of an immortal soul that would find a body, but remains faithful to the Semitic view proposed by Daniel, a view that he himself had adopted in 1 Thessalonians: what is raised is the human being in its entirety and not just in its body. First, let us note that Paul does not speak of the resurrection of "the body" but of "the dead" (15:12, 21, 42); it is "the dead" who are raised as in 1 Thessalonians 4:16. Besides, Paul uses the locution "those who have fallen asleep" (15:6, 18, 20, 51; NJB) as he had done in 1 Thessalonians 4:13, 14, 15 (NJB) and as Daniel had done in 12:2. Later on, he will no longer make use of this locution because, as we shall see, he will have adopted a way of thinking more Greek than Semitic. Indeed, this expression fits the theme inherited from Daniel, according to which it is the whole human being who "falls asleep" and rises only at the resurrection; but it is absolutely unsuited to the Greek view of an immortal soul which will continue to live with God. Is it possible for anyone to "sleep" when enjoying the divine presence with Christ? And how could Paul have written that if there is no resurrection, "those who have fallen asleep in Christ are utterly lost [*apólonto*]" (15:18; NJB) had he thought that at death, their souls are blissfully with God.

c) One last argument is supplied us in verses 12 and 32b. While writing his thoughts on the resurrection, Paul wants to refute the skepticism of certain Christians who contend that there is no resurrection of the dead (v. 12). These people do not deny the resurrection of the body, but that of the dead. Paul ironically endorses their position in verse 32b, "If the dead are not raised, 'Let us eat and drink for tomorrow we die'" (see Isa 22:13). It matters little whether the people Paul has in mind are Epicureans or Sadducees converted to Christianity. In their view, the soul is not immortal, and there is nothing after death; therefore, no punishment can reach us once our earthly life has come to an end. So, let us enjoy life right now! In answering them, what would be the use of invoking a resurrection of just the body? Paul would do better to reply that they had an immortal soul which could be punished after physical death. Much more radically, what Paul wants to do is prove that the whole human being, after disappearing for a time, will one day come back to life and therefore could then incur punishment.[29]

Before undertaking the detailed analysis of Paul's text, it is important to clarify the perspective in which he places himself: it is the same as in 1 Thessalonians, the Semitic perspective he had drawn from Daniel. At the time of death, when God withdraws the vital breath, the whole human being falls asleep in the dust of earth and waits for the day when Christ will recall him or her to life. There is no question of an immortal soul being reunited with a body.

The How of the Resurrection

Let us now go to the core of the subject by attempting to understand how Paul envisages our resurrection. His thought unfolds as follows:[30]

> Introduction: the problem is posed (v. 35).
>   How the resurrection happens;

---

[29] We endorse what Puech has written in *La Croyance,* 267: "Paul's language–'to fall asleep, to wake up, to live again'–borrows from Semitic anthropology and is in harmony with the most traditional teaching of faith in resurrection. Paul envisages the resurrection of the whole human being, that of the body, v. 35, and not in the Platonic sense of body opposed to soul." Then he refers readers to Dahl, *Resurrection.* But he does not give the exact meaning of the word "body" nor does he say how it should be translated.

[30] We propose this plan in order to facilitate our explanation. There could probably be other plans.

two examples to illustrate it:
 the sowing (vv. 36-38),
 the diversity of beings (vv. 39-41).
So is it with the resurrection (vv. 42-44a).
Christ is the principle of the resurrection (vv. 44b-49).
The perspective widens: the living and the dead (vv. 50-54).
Conclusion: death will be definitively overcome (vv. 55-57).

So, the problem is posed in verse 35: "But someone will ask, 'How are the dead raised? With what kind of body do they come?'"

a) Two examples are proposed to help readers get some idea of the mystery.
 – The first is taken from agriculture:

> 36. Fool! What you sow does not come to life unless it dies.
> 37. As for what you sow, you do not sow the body that is to be, but a bare seed, perhaps of wheat or of some other grain.
> 38. But God gives it a body as he has chosen, and to each kind of seed its own body.

The analogy between sowing and resurrection appears in verse 36: in both cases, it is a mystery of death and life. The seed placed in the ground must first disintegrate and decay before giving birth to a green plant; in the same way, the corpse placed in the ground must first putrefy (cf. John 12:24) before giving birth to a new being. But, and this is the important point, Paul immediately insists on the fact that what will sprout from the earth is not the seed that was sown, *but a completely different being,* a plant. Of course, it is God who effects the transformation in accordance with the nature of each plant. Readers can already understand that the corpse buried in the earth is not what comes back to life, but a different being whose nature must be described. This is what Paul now does.
 – The second example points to the diversity of the beings composing the cosmos:

> 39. Not all flesh is alike, but there is one flesh for human beings, another for animals, another for birds, and another for fish.

> 40. There are both heavenly bodies and earthly bodies, but the glory [the radiance][31] of the heavenly is one thing, and that of the earthly is another.
> 41. There is one glory of the sun, and another glory of the moon, and another glory of the stars; indeed, star differs from star in glory.

Paul insists here on the diversity existing between beings,[32] whether they live on earth or move in the heavens. But the essential difference is between the earthly beings and the heavenly beings; this is the difference that Paul develops in what follows. At this point, by combining the two comparisons, readers are able to understand that there exists a difference of *nature* between what is placed in the ground, the corpse, and what will be raised, the risen being. An earthly being is buried in the earth and a completely different being will rise, comparable to the stars shining in the sky.

b) Paul now draws the practical conclusion from the two examples he has just given:[33]

> 42. So it is with the resurrection of the dead. What is sown is perishable, what is raised is imperishable.
> 43. It is sown in dishonor, it is raised in glory. It is sown in weakness, it is raised in power.
> 44a. It is sown a [psychic] body, it is raised a spiritual body.

What is sown, what is deposited in the earth, the corpse, is a corruptible being not having the strength to resist corruption,

[31] The Greek word *doxa* has here the sense of luminous "brilliance," but we translate by "glory," which is a quasi-technical term to designate the state of celestial entities which participate in the divine "glory." We shall have to be more precise on this important point.

[32] In v. 39, the word we are translating by "flesh," *sarx*, is a synonym of *sōma*, both of which render the Hebrew *basar; basar* is often translated by *sarx* in the Septuagint and is applicable to any creature inasmuch as it is subject to corruption (see Gen 6:3; Isa 40:6-8).

[33] The translation of this passage is difficult because Paul uses Greek words with a twofold meaning which are impossible to render in English.

an object of horror when it begins to decompose. What will get up, that is, rise (the Greek verb has both meanings), is an incorruptible being glorious and powerful enough to overcome corruption.

The last contrast, expressed by Paul in verse 44a, is difficult to understand. In reality, it is a link with the following development, which it introduces. We shall attempt to discern its meaning only after explaining verses 45-49.

Christ, Principle of the Resurrection

In verses 45-49, Paul presents the resurrection as a new creation whose life-giving principle is no other than Christ, the new Adam:[34]

> 44b. If there is a psychic body, there is also a spiritual body.
> 45. Thus it is written: Became the first human, Adam, a living being, [became] the last Adam, life-giving spirit.
> 46. But there was not first the spiritual, but the psychic, then the spiritual.
> 47. The first human, born of earth, is of dust; the second human is from heaven.
> 48. As was the human of dust, so are those who are of the dust; and as is the human of heaven, so are those who are of heaven.
> 49. And as we have borne the image of the human of dust, so will we bear the image of the human from heaven.

The preceding development ended with this opposition, "It is sown a [psychic] body, it is raised a spiritual body." Paul now explains how he understands these two adjectives, psychic and spiritual.

a) The formula "thus it is written" refers to the text of Genesis 2:7, describing the creation of the first human being, but here we are encountering problems of translation. The Hebrew text has, "Then YHWH God formed the human, dust [drawn] from the earth, and breathed into its nostrils a breath

---

[34] We are translating very literally, taking into account the text of LXX Gen 2:7, which Paul will use.

of life and the human became a living being." But Paul cites this passage according to the Septuagint, which is a bit different, "And God formed the human, dust [drawn] from the earth, and breathed on its face a breath of life and the human became a living being." Let us see in detail the allusions to Genesis in Paul's development.

– In verse 45a, Paul begins by explicitly quoting the end of the Genesis text, simply adding two glosses "first" and "Adam": "became the [first] human [Adam] a living being." Translations are often erroneous. To say "living being," the Hebrew text uses the word *nefesh*, which has numerous meanings in the Bible and here effectively has the rather vague sense of "living being." The Septuagint ordinarily translates the Hebrew word by the Greek *psuchē*, whose meaning can vary depending on the context. But here we confront the same problem as with the word *sōma*. It is true that *psuchē* can mean "soul," especially when it is opposed to the body. But this is a philosophical meaning; in common parlance, the word means first of all "life" (a very frequent meaning in the New Testament, particularly the Gospels), then, by derivation, "a living being, a person" (see Liddell–Scott, *Lexicon*). Paul is fully aware of this latter meaning, well attested in the New Testament (Rom 13:1; Acts 2:41, 43; see also Rom 2:9; 2 Cor 12:15), and it is obviously how he understands the word when he cites Genesis 2:7 according to the Septuagint. Therefore, we must translate, as in Genesis, "and the human became a living being," and not "a living soul." We shall see later how verse 44a must be understood with this meaning of the word *psuchē*.

– In verse 45b, Paul continues by saying that "the last Adam [became] a life-giving spirit" *(pneuma zōopoioun)*. Here again, we risk being misled by the translation "life-giving spirit." It is true that the word *pneuma* can mean "spirit," but its first and most habitual meaning is "breath," either that of the wind or that of any living being. Let us again come back to the text of Genesis 2:7 where it is said that God breathed into the human's nostrils a "breath [*nishmat*] of life." The Septuagint translates this by *pnoēn zōēs*, which means, as in the Hebrew, "breath of life." But in the Hellenistic Jewish tradition, when one quoted Genesis 2:7, one tended to replace the word *pnoē* by the more frequent term *pneuma*, which, as was noted above, had the same meaning. This substitution is current in Philo of Alexandria and is also found, for instance, in Wisdom 15:11, which, alluding to Genesis 2:7, replaces the locution *pnoēn zōēs* by *pneuma zōtikon*, "life-giving breath." We are close to Paul's expression *pneuma zōopoiun*, which should be translated, not "life-giving spirit," but "life-giving breath" since Paul is citing Genesis 2:7. For Paul, Christ acts like this "breath" which God had breathed on the human's face to give it life.

– One last allusion to the text of Genesis is in verse 47, "The first human, born of earth [*ek gēs*], is of dust [*choikos*]." This is obviously a repetition of the expression in Genesis according to which God fashioned the "human, dust [drawn] from the earth [*choun apo tēs gēs*]" (LXX).

b) In what way does Paul use this passage from Genesis to explain the resurrection? By developing a twofold opposition, one between Adam and Christ (v. 47), the other between the state of humanity before and after the eschatological event (vv. 48-50).

The first human, Adam, was "dust,[35] [drawn] from the earth"; in other words, the human had been formed from the dust of the earth, its nature was to be "dust" according to Genesis 2:7. On the contrary, the second Adam, that is, Christ, is "from heaven." This expression does not just mean that Christ comes from heaven; more deeply, it means that Christ is, *by nature*, "heavenly." The parallelism between the two characters demands it. This echoes the opposition Paul established in verse 40: there are earthly beings and heavenly beings. One could then have understood simply that there are beings that live on earth and beings that live in heaven. But in fact, owing to the opposition stated in verse 47, one must interpret the sentence in the sense that there are beings made of earth, "born of dust," and beings made of a heavenly substance.

---

[35] As is shown in what follows, we give a particular meaning to this word.

In verses 48-49, Paul is now able to shed more light on the mystery of the resurrection by explaining that there will be the same opposition between the state of human beings before the eschatological event and their state afterwards: "As was the man of dust, so are those who are of the dust; and as is the man of heaven, so are those who are of heaven. Just as we have borne the image of the man of dust [cf. Gen 5:3], we will also bear the image of the man of heaven [cf. Gen 1:27]." To come back to the initial comparisons Paul gives, a being of dust and therefore corruptible and without honor is buried, a being made of heavenly substance, incorruptible and pervaded by divine glory, is raised (see vv. 42-43).

c) We can now come back to the opposition stated in v. 44a, whose translation is difficult. Let us quote it with the Greek terms we shall presently explain: "It is sown as a *sōma psuchikon*, it rises as a *sōma pneumatikon*." We have already said that the word *sōma* has to be rendered, not by "body" (opposed to soul), but by the rather vague term of "being."[36] And now let us make clear the meaning of the two adjectives.

The second one is derived from the noun *pneuma*, whose first and most common meaning is "breath," as we said above. The perspective here is eschatological: what is under discussion is risen humanity. Now Paul is about to explain in the following verses that humanity rises by the power of Christ acting as *pneuma zōopoiun*, as "life-giving breath." There is no doubt about the sense of the second part of verse 44: what will stand up, what will rise, is a being which Christ, "life-giving breath," has transformed. The risen being is called *pneumatikon* because it is transformed by Christ, "life-giving breath." But then how should we translate the expression *sōma pneumatikon* to preserve its profound meaning? It would be best to use the English adjective that is a mere transcription of the Greek, "pneumatic." Many English medical terms begin with "pneuma-," all having to do with the lungs, the organs of respiration.

---

[36] But inasmuch as it is composed of matter, visible and tangible.

What about the first expression, *sōma psuchikon*? The adjective is derived from the Greek noun *psuchē*. After all the explanations he has just given, it is obvious that Paul thinks of the text of Genesis 2:7 (LXX), where it is said that by receiving the "breath of life," the human became *psuchēn zōsan*, a "living being" (v. 45). However, from the viewpoint of meaning, it is impossible to regard as equivalent the noun *psuchē* of verse 45 and the adjective *psuchikon* of verse 44. We are led to recognize that in verse 44, Paul's vocabulary is influenced by that of Stoic philosophy with its distinction between "body" and "soul," without the soul's being conceived of as immortal. What is buried in the earth is a "psychic body," a being made of body and soul but subject to corruption and destined for total disappearance.

So, here is how Paul sees the resurrection of humanity. A "psychic being," that is, a being made up of a body and a soul—neither immortal—is buried in the earth. This being is only "dust" (Gen 2:7) and must go back to dust (Gen 3:19). Everything disappears. In a relatively near future, there will rise a being completely transformed by the action of Christ, "life-giving breath." This being will no longer be made of "dust"; it will no longer be "of dust," but will be endowed with a heavenly, incorruptible substance, as if transformed into light (glory). Later on, we shall come back to what Paul understood by this.

The Perspective Widens

In verses 50-54, Paul widens his horizon and envisions the destiny of those who will still be alive at the time of the eschatological event; he had done the same thing in 1 Thessalonians, following the prophet Daniel:

> 50. What I am saying, brothers and sisters, is this: flesh and blood cannot inherit the kingdom of God, nor does the perishable inherit the imperishable.
> 51. Listen, I will tell you a mystery! We will not all die, but we will all be changed,
> 52. in a moment, in the twinkling of an eye, at the last trumpet. For the trumpet will sound, and the dead will be raised imperishable, and we will be changed.

53. For this perishable body must put on imperishability, and this mortal body must put on immortality.
54. When this perishable body puts on imperishability, and this mortal body puts on immortality, then the saying that is written will be fulfilled: "Death has been swallowed up in victory."

To make the transition with the following development, Paul poses the principle that "flesh and blood cannot inherit incorruptibility." In the Bible, the word "flesh" often designates humanity inasmuch as it is subject to corruption (see Gen 3:6; Isa 40:8). In Paul's time, the expression in use was rather "flesh and blood," but the meaning was the same. Here is Paul's reasoning: the whole of humanity is corruptible by nature. But God's reign will include only incorruptible beings. In order to be able to participate in this reign, we must "put on incorruptibility." So at the time of the eschatological event, thanks to the action of Christ, "life-giving breath," not only the dead will rise incorruptible, but all those still alive will be radically transformed and their being of dust from the earth will be changed into a being made of heavenly substance. Later on, in Romans 8:18-23, Paul will even envision a radical transformation of the whole cosmos, which will be delivered from "bondage to decay."

The Eschatological World

We have seen that in 1 Thessalonians, Paul thought of a reign of God being established on earth. The eschatological event would be the return of Christ to earth, his parousia. Paul's view is different now. Indeed, in the entire development of verses 35-56, he no longer speaks of Christ's parousia, although it is Christ's presence that must effect the transformation of all human beings. Did he change his mind concerning the place where the reign of God will be realized?

For Paul, as we have seen, humanity as a whole will have taken leave of its nature of "dust" to put on another purely "heavenly" nature. Not only shall we be in heaven, but our substance will be heavenly. Now let us look again at what Paul suggests in verses 40-41: we shall all rise as celestial beings, that is, like the sun, the moon, and the stars. Does he not want to say that we shall be similar to the stars? To become convinced of this possibility, we refer readers to André-Jean Festugière's writings,[37] from which we give some excerpts here.

Numerous funerary inscriptions affirm that at death, the soul, separated from the body, goes to dwell in the world of stars. Let us quote the end of one of the most interesting, discovered in Kékira and dating back to the second century C.E., "At the age of forty, having left my body in the earth, I went to the sky shining with stars" (p. 148). Another example is this inscription in Thásos, "Advised by the gods, the soul went to be near the stars and participates in the choir of the blessed" (p. 151). Festugière explains this statement: "This idea is but the development of the belief in the fusion of the soul with the divine ether. Besides, because the ancients believed in the divinity of stars, whose movement they thought was due to the influence of these divine souls, by going to live in a star the soul went to the abode of the gods" (p. 150).

According to most of these inscriptions, it is only the soul that rejoins the world of stars in order to dwell there. But other testimonies show a more precise belief: after death, humans are transformed into stars, without any distinction between their souls and their bodies. Thus this funerary inscription in Amorgós, "Do not weep, mother, for why cry? Rather venerate me for I have become the divine star that appears when evening comes" (p. 150). This is a very old idea since it is attested as a popular and apparently widespread belief in Aristophanes' *Peace* (5.832–838), where the author records this dialogue between a slave and his master Trygaeus.

> *Slave:* So also it isn't true after all what they say, that when we die we become stars in the sky?
> *Trygaeus:* It's very true indeed.
> *Slave:* And who's a star up there now?

[37] Festugière, *L'idéal,* 146–151.

> *Trygaeus:* Ion of Chios, the man who years ago, down here, composed *The Star of Dawning.* When he came up there, right away, everyone called the Star of Dawning![38]

Festugière introduces this series of texts by saying, "It would be easy to demonstrate the philosophical origin of this type of inscription, so let us add a few testimonies in favor of astral immortality, a belief–inspired by Neo-Pythagoreanism–that became widespread at the beginning of the Christian era" (p. 149).

This conception of the celestial future of humanity was not unknown to Jewish thought. We read in 4 Maccabees (17:5)–about which we shall speak later–concerning the mother of the seven brothers tortured by Antiochus Epiphanes, "The moon in heaven, with the stars, does not stand so august as you, who, after lighting the way of your star-like seven sons to piety, stand in honor before God and are firmly set in heaven with them." In the present text, the words "you are set" translate the Greek verb *estērisai,* but some commentators think this is a correction replacing the difficult *ēsterisai,* "you were changed into a star," a very rare verb but known to Plutarch (*Moralia* 888 D).

Thus, we can see the evolution of Paul's thought concerning the place where the eschatological reign will be established. In 1 Thessalonians, it was on earth, an earth already transformed, but still on earth. The beginning of this earthly reign would be marked by Christ's parousia, his entry into his terrestrial reign. In 1 Corinthians 15:22-28, this rule will still be established on earth and will be inaugurated by the parousia, but it will have a limited duration. A day will come when Christ will hand over the reign to his Father, when death will be definitively conquered. In 1 Corinthians 15:51-54, there is no longer any earthly reign and the term "parousia" is completely abandoned by Paul. The eschatological reign is in the heavens; here the stars move, which were considered living beings, according to a conception rather prevalent at the time. Later on, in Colossians 3:1-4, the reign will be in God.

[38] Aristophanes, *Peace,* ed. and trans. Alan H. Sommerstein (Chicago, 1985) 81.

Part Two

THE IMMORTALITY OF THE SOUL

---- 1 ----

The Biblical Preparations

As the Jewish world grew receptive to Greek ideas, it came to conceive of the victory of humanity over death in terms, no longer of "resurrection," but of "immortality." Already known in Orphism, the notion of immortality received its philosophical configuration from Plato in the beginning of the fourth century B.C.E. A human person is no longer seen as a psychosomatic whole whose entire conscious life would originate in his or her physical elements but as a duality of a soul and a body, distinct and separable realities. Of these two elements, only the body is corruptible: formed from earth, it dissolves into earth at the time of death. As for the soul, it is immortal by nature. It existed even before coming to inhabit a body. At death, it leaves its body, either to join another body or, if it has become pure enough, to go to the world of Ideas, the world of the divine. The soul is the principle and center of the whole of human conscious life: intelligence, will, feelings; therefore, the entire personality of any human being resides in his or her soul. In a certain sense, one can say that human beings do not die since, thanks to their souls, they continue to be fully alive after leaving their bodies. Death is but an appearance. Lastly, let us note that for Plato, the idea of a resurrection of the body was unthinkable. Because of its earthy origin, the body is attracted to the earth, the world of the senses; it impedes the full development of the soul's intellectual faculties. When the soul, once purified, has joined the world of Ideas, there is no more question of its being reunited to the body in which it has lived as in a prison.

This very sketchy presentation of Plato's theory will be sufficient to allow us to understand how certain currents of thought among Jews, and later on Christians, envisaged the question of our victory over death. First, we shall see that a number of biblical narratives prepared certain Jewish circles[1] to adopt this notion of immortality. Afterwards, we shall discover how, through a compromise with traditional beliefs, this notion was accepted in chapters 102–104 of the apocryphal book of Enoch, written about the year 100 B.C.E., and in the canonical[2] book of Wisdom, composed half a century later. Finally, we shall see how, in 2 Corinthians, Paul himself combined Platonic and Semitic ideas.

The Case of the Patriarch Enoch

Genesis 5 gives "the list of the descendants of Adam," which contains the names of the patriarchs who succeeded one another from Adam to the Flood. A short stereotyped notice is devoted to each of the ancestors. As an example, here is the one concerning Kenan: "When Kenan had lived seventy years, he became the father of Mahalalel. Kenan lived after the birth of Mahalalel eight hundred and forty years, and had other sons and daughters. Thus all the days of Kenan were nine hundred and ten years, and he died" (vv. 12-14). The account of each of the patriarchs living before the Flood ends with the statement "and he died." Only Enoch is an exception to the rule. His notice follows the stereotypical form except at the end; instead of "and he died," we read, "Enoch walked with God; then he was no more, because God took him" (v. 24; cf. Sir 44:16). During his whole life,

---

[1] All the texts, either biblical or not, have been assembled by Frey, "La vie."

[2] It is not canonical for Protestants who adhere to the canon of the Jewish Bible.

Enoch strove to live in accord with God's will, and this is why, instead of dying like the other patriarchs, he was "taken," that is, "carried off" by God.[3]

Jewish tradition has often commented on this text from Genesis, which it always understood as meaning that Enoch had escaped death. Let us cite only one passage from the book of Jubilees, an apocryphal Jewish work written either at the beginning or, more probably, at the end of the second century B.C.E. Angels speak about the patriarch Enoch in these terms, "And he was taken from the midst of the children of humanity and we led him to the garden of Eden in majesty and honor, and there, he wrote down the condemnation and the judgment of the world" (4:23).[4] For his part, the Jewish historian Flavius Josephus writes, "Now he [Enoch], when he had lived three hundred and sixty-five years, departed, and went to God."[5]

Later on, we shall go into more detail concerning the way Jewish tradition was able to understand this victory over death in the case of Enoch.[6]

The Case of the Prophet Elijah

Another biblical character knew a fate similar to Enoch's: the prophet Elijah. The second book of Kings narrates the end of his earthly life in this way: Elijah was walking with his disciple Elisha beyond the Jordan. "As they continued walking and talking, a chariot of fire and horses

---

[3] On the Babylonian origin of the theme, which would have been known to the Hebrews at the time of the Exile, see Grelot, "La Légende."

[4] Allusion to the apocryphal book of Enoch which we shall meet again in the following chapter.

[5] Flavius Josephus, *Ant.* 3.3.4.

[6] Grelot, "La légende," 210, very judiciously writes, *"Therefore, a literary current exists in which the doctrine of retribution is developed from the legend of Enoch itself.* It can be traced from the priestly document to the books of Wisdom and 1 Enoch, with, in-between, Pss 49 and 73, which give only a hint of it."

of fire separated the two of them, and Elijah ascended in a whirlwind into heaven" (2:11). He had just told his disciple, who had asked him to inherit a double share of his spirit, "You have asked a hard thing; yet, if you see me as I am taken from you, it will be granted you; if not, it will not." Elijah is "taken" by God exactly as Enoch had been (the Hebrew verb is the same). Although he is no longer on earth, he is still alive in a mysterious place. And this is why the prophet Malachi sees him coming back on earth to prepare the great eschatological judgment: "Lo, I will send you the prophet Elijah before the great and terrible day of the LORD comes" (4:5). Jesus' disciples will echo this belief when they query, "Why do the scribes say that Elijah must come first?" (Mark 9:11).

Enoch and Elijah are the only two persons about whom the Bible explicitly says that they left the earth without going through death. But there were others whom popular opinion held as still alive. For instance, we read in 2 Maccabees 15:13-14, "Then in the same fashion another appeared, distinguished by his grey hair and dignity, and of marvelous majesty and authority. And Onias spoke, saying, 'This is a man who loves the family of Israel and prays much for the people and the holy city–Jeremiah, the prophet of God.'" That Jeremiah can intercede with God in favor of his people proves that he is still alive.

Death Is Vanquished

These biblical texts do not oblige us to believe that their authors would have adopted the Platonic idea of a distinction between the incorruptible soul and the corruptible body. Enoch, Elijah, and Jeremiah are taken from the earth with what we now call their bodies. This is obvious in the case of Jeremiah since in the text above, he appears in human form with his "white hair." The same must be true of Enoch and Elijah. But the important thing is that they left the earth without dying. Thus, death is conquered. There will be expressions used to designate this phenomenon: "they did not see death" and "they did not taste death." For example, concerning the advent of the Messiah, the author of 4 Esdras says, "And the men who have been taken up, who have not tasted death from their birth, shall appear" (6:26). Likewise, the author of Hebrews alludes in 11:5 to the rapture of Enoch in these terms,[7] "By faith Enoch was taken so that he did not experience death; and he was not found because God had taken him." The two expressions mentioned above are found also in John's Gospel (8:51-52).

In the Jewish tradition, some persons favored by God left the earth without dying, retaining their physical integrity. According to Plato, all humans leave the earth, thanks to their immortal souls, and their death is only apparent. Even though it might not accept the distinction between soul and body, biblical tradition certainly prepared Jewish thinking to adopt Platonic ideas about our victory over death.

We reserve the study of Psalms 49 and 73 until later, after we have analyzed the book of Enoch and the book of Wisdom.

[7] The author follows the Septuagint as does the author of Wisdom (part 2, ch. 3, p. 64).

------ 2 ------

The Apocryphal Book of Enoch

— (Chs. 102–104) —

Many scholars have noted the similarity between the apocryphal book of Enoch and the book of Wisdom.[8] Therefore, it will not be useless to analyze in passing the way in which the work attributed to the patriarch Enoch envisages the question of our victory over death.

But such an analysis is difficult. Up to the discoveries in the caves of Qumran, it was known in its entirety only in an Ethiopic translation;[9] there was also a Greek translation of chapters 1–32:89 (partially), and 97:6–107.[10] It was known that the book had been originally written in Aramaic, which was confirmed by the deciphering of the very many fragments found at Qumran.[11] In its present state, the book is an assemblage of various documents composed at different times. Thus, according to Josef T. Milik, one should distinguish, in chronological order, the following sections: 1. The "Astronomical Book" (chs. 78–82) is a sort of calendar going back to the fourth century B.C.E. (fragments discovered at Qumran could be dated from the end of the third century or

---

[8] We refer readers especially to Grelot, "L'eschatologie."
[9] See Charles, *Enoch;* Black, *Enoch*.
[10] Black, *Apocalypsis*.
[11] Edited by Milik, *Books*.

the beginning of the second century B.C.E.). 2. The "Book of the Watchers" (chs. 1–36) would have been written in the middle of the third century B.C.E. 3. The "Book of Dreams" (chs. 83–90) was composed about 164 B.C.E. 4. A "Letter of Enoch"[12] (chs. 91–105) was written about 100 B.C.E. 5. Chapters 106–107 would be more recent. 6. As to chapters 37–82, of which no fragments have been found in Qumran, they might be a later Christian composition, a hypothesis that is contested today.

We have no intention of undertaking a complete study of this composite work, but shall limit ourselves to chapters 102–104, which can best shed direct light on the question of our victory over death found in Wisdom.[13]

General Theme and Structure of the Passage

The dominant idea developed in this passage from Enoch is the following: Of what benefit is it for the righteous to observe the divine law? During their earthly life, they encounter only difficulties while sinners thrive and have a good time. At death, both righteous and sinners go down to Sheol. The latter do not fail to taunt the former by reminding them of this fact, borne out by experience. However, the just are on the winning side–even though they are in Sheol for the present, along with the impious–because a day will come when God will vindicate them. At the time of the judgment, they will leave Sheol in order to enjoy unmitigated bliss with God, whereas the sinners will remain there and be prey to horrible sufferings.

This overall theme is developed in four steps which correspond to one another two by two.[14] 1. In the first section

[12] More commonly called "Book of the Exhortation and the Curse."

[13] In the following analysis, we shall use the text established by Black, *Apocalypsis*. [The English translation of Enoch is that of Black, *Enoch;* all emphases are the author's.]

[14] See Nickelsburg, *Resurrection*. See also, with more detailed notes, his article "Apocalyptic," 319.

(102:4–103:4), the author speaks of the righteous who have gone down to Sheol after their death, and he exhorts them to have confidence (102:4-5); then he describes the mocking words spoken to them by the evildoers who for the time being share their lot (vv. 6-11); then, in a still veiled way, he hints at their future happiness (103:1-4). 2. In the second section (103:5-8), the writer addresses the wicked who also have gone down to Sheol. He begins by warning them of what is in store for them (v. 5a); then he repeats the taunts they direct at the righteous (vv. 5b-6). He continues by threatening them with the punishments reserved for them (vv. 7-8). 3. In the third section (103:9–104:6), the writer speaks to the righteous who are still alive. After a solemn warning (103:9a), he lets us hear the righteous lamenting their present misfortune (vv. 9b-15). Then he depicts the wonderful destiny God has planned for them in the near future (104:1-6). 4. The fourth section (104:7-8), which concerns the sinners who are still alive, has the same structure as the preceding: solemn admonition to the impious (v. 7a), who take pride in their lives (v. 7b), thus making a great mistake (v. 8). Verses 9-13 are the conclusion of the whole passage.

The Final Destiny of Humans

a) Let us first observe that whoever authored this section of the book of Enoch has adopted an anthropology that is Greek rather than Semitic in character. This is obvious from the beginning of the passage (102:4-5):

> Fear not, *souls* of the righteous who have died,
> And grieve not because your *souls* have gone down to Sheol in tribulation,
> And that, in your lives, your *body of flesh* did not obtain [a reward] according to your piety. . . .

During their earthly lives, human beings are made up of soul and body. At the moment of death, the soul is separated from the body and goes down by itself to Sheol. Similarly, in 102:11, the sinners rail against the just by saying, "But they perished and became as though they had not been; / And *their souls* descended into Sheol in tribulation." When, to counteract this sarcasm, Enoch wants to comfort the righteous by promising them a final blissful destiny, he tells them (103:1-4):

> . . . I swear to you–
> That I understand the following mystery
> For I have read [on] the tablets of heaven
>
> . . . . .
>
> That all good things and joy and honour are prepared
> And written down for the *spirits* of the righteous dead,
>
> . . . . .
>
> And the *spirits* of you righteous who have died will live and
>   rejoice and be glad,
> And *their spirit* shall not perish. . . .

Likewise, concerning the wicked, Enoch predicts (103:7-8):

> Know that *their souls* will be made to descend into Sheol,
> And they shall be afflicted in great tribulation, and in dark-
>   ness and in the toils of death and in a blazing fire.
> And to the great judgment *their souls* will come,
> And the great judgment shall be for all generations for ever.

Therefore, only the souls, gone down to Sheol at the end of their earthly lives, are destined to be given the joy that is prepared for them or to suffer endless torments.

b) What will be the fate of the righteous? In 103:2-4, Enoch remains vague and only promises the realization of what is still hidden, what is still only a "mystery": great goods, joy, and honor. But in chapter 104, he is far more explicit: "Be of good courage, for aforetime you were worn down by evils and afflictions, but now you shall shine and appear as the lights of heaven, and the portals of heaven shall be opened unto you" (v. 2). The souls of the just, who are for the present waiting in Sheol, will soon enter heaven where they shall shine like stars. Therefore, Enoch here repeats Daniel 12:3, but he gives to this text a different thrust. We have seen that for Daniel, the "wise," in charge of teaching others are the ones who "shall shine like the brightness of the sky"; this means that their teaching will be welcomed by people. Daniel, who thought that humans rise in their psychosomatic totality, did not foresee a radical transformation of the conditions of life on earth. Neither did Enoch, but yet his outlook is different. Since only the souls enter heaven, he can say that they will shine like the stars of heaven without, for all that, postulating that "matter" will be transformed into "light."

A little farther along (104:6), Enoch will again allude to this entrance of the souls into heaven; he says to the just who are still living on earth, "But now fear not, you righteous, when you see the sinners growing strong and prospering . . . for you shall become companions of the angels of heaven."

As for the sinners, not only are they condemned to remain in Sheol, but they will endure there eternal suffering:

> Know that their souls will be made to descend into Sheol, and they shall be afflicted in great tribulation, and in darkness and in the toils of death and in a blazing fire. And to the great judgment their souls will come, and the great judgment shall be for all generations for ever. Woe to you for you shall have no peace (103:7-8).

c) Therefore, here is how we can summarize the final destiny of human beings according to Enoch 102–104. At death, the souls of all humans, just and sinners alike, are separated from their bodies and go down to Sheol where they await God's judgment. On that day, the souls of the just will leave Sheol in order to enter heaven, where, in the company of angels, they will shine like stars. As for the souls of evildoers, they will remain in Sheol and be afflicted by great suffering.

It is clear that the body is absent from this perspective, as several authors have rightly observed. Thus, Robert H. Charles has written, "The focus of interest has passed from a material world to a spiritual world and the Messianic kingdom is no longer the goal and the hope of the just. Their faith can be satisfied only by a blissful immortality, in heaven itself."[15] Similarly, Pierre Grelot writes:

[15] Charles, *Enoch*, cviii–cvix, 260 (n. 6).

In any case, one conclusion is inescapable. If one leaves aside Enoch's parables, one finds in the rest of the work and in the book of Jubilees, which closely resembles it, an eschatology whose essential points are the following: individual retribution after this life is clearly affirmed; its realization is linked with the traditional theme of the divine Judgment; it supposes the immortality of the soul or the spirit (both words being understood as does Semitic anthropology);[16] it excludes the resurrection of the body.[17]

And Milik writes: "The blissful afterlife of the just is therefore essentially spiritual, concerning only their souls and spirits (103:3-4). In a parallel fashion, the sinners' souls will suffer for all eternity (102:11; 103:7-8)."[18] Let us also quote George W.E. Nickelsburg:

> Nowhere in these chapters does the author speak of the resurrection of the body. Even though he mentions the fact that the bodies of the just have been mistreated during their life (102:5), he does not say that these bodies will obtain a new life. Their spirits are what will live and will not perish and will receive the good things prepared for them.[19]

A Resurrection of the Body?

Could the author of Enoch have envisaged, in spite of everything, a resurrection of the body? Some authors have thought so by basing themselves on a few texts cited in the preceding sections.[20]

For instance, they rely for proof on 100:5 in which it is said, "The pious will sleep a pleasant sleep." Like Daniel, the author of Enoch would be speaking here of the sleep of death, which would entail, still as in Daniel, a future resurrection. Let us remark first that even if this were the meaning of 100:5, it would not necessarily imply a resurrection of the

---

[16] This parenthesis seems contestable to us.

[17] Grelot, "L'eschatologie," 123.

[18] Milik, *Books*, 54.

[19] Nickelsburg, *Resurrection*, 123.

[20] See, among others, Puech, *La Croyance*, 114–116.

body. But more radically, is the author speaking of the sleep of death? Everything happens on earth. The just are the butt of persecution on the part of sinners. But there will come a day when God will reduce the latter to powerlessness and will protect those faithful to God:

> And [God] will set a guard from the holy angels over all the righteous and holy:
> They will guard them as the apple of an eye,
>
> . . . . .
>
> And thereafter the pious will sleep a pleasant sleep,
> And there will no longer be one to terrify them (100:5).

This is not the sleep of death, as numerous commentators think. Enoch simply says that the righteous will be able to sleep in peace without fearing the persecution of their enemies.[21] This is what the prophet Hosea promised in the past: "I will make for you a covenant on that day with the wild animals . . . and I will make you lie down in safety" (2:18).

Can we find more solid ground in the sentences found in 91:10, "And the righteous shall arise from their sleep . . . ," and 92:3, "And the righteous shall awake from sleep . . ."? These texts would speak of a resurrection of the dead, implying that they would find bodies again. But these two sentences are part of a well-defined whole. We have here a classical apocalyptic theme: there will come a time when impiety will dominate the earth and the evildoers will persecute the just. But let these be patient, a day will come when God will set up a judgment against the impious and will restore justice on earth. It is then that "the righteous shall arise from their sleep." If one wanted to understand the expression in the sense of a resurrection,[22] this resurrection would leave the

---

[21] Thus Stemberger, *Der Leib,* 41, "Here, the image of sleep is nothing more than the symbol of the security of the righteous on earth as soon as sin is destroyed."

[22] We think that 91:10 and 92:3 say only that the just will awaken (cf. 1 Thess 5:6) to lead a life full of wisdom, as the whole context indicates; see Stemberger, *Der Leib,* 40–42. In order not to

just on earth, an earth purified from all evil. The perspective is that of Daniel 12:1-2, and *everything happens on earth;* this is explicitly said in 91:5, 6, 7, 9. Now, according to chapters 102–104, when God delivers the souls of the just from Sheol, it will be *to have them enter into heaven,* into the light, with the angels. We are here in the presence of two fragments artificially joined by the redactor of Enoch, two fragments offering two perspectives, different and incompatible.[23]

Platonism Influenced by Judaism

It is easy to see how the author of Enoch blends Greek and Jewish ideas. He is close to Platonism in the acceptance that human beings are composed of a body and a soul. At the time of death, the soul is separated from the body and will live on alone. In a certain sense, it is immortal. But the author corrects Platonism on an important point, borrowed from Jewish ideas. For Plato, the soul that is sufficiently purified on earth goes directly to rejoin the world of Ideas, the world of the divine. In contrast, for the author of Enoch there is an intermediary state: the souls of the just first go down to Sheol, where they wait for the day God will remember them in order to lead them into heaven in the company of the angels. This theme of the descent into Sheol is obviously taken from Judaism, but with a profound modification. The righteous do not go down to Sheol as evanescent shades deprived of life, but as souls having kept intact their personality.

And whereas for Daniel, the eschatological kingdom was to be established on earth, for the author of Enoch, it is established in heaven, therefore, with God.

---

give any opportunity to criticism, we have not taken this hypothesis into account.

[23] According to Grelot, "L'eschatologie," 121, "Such a resurrection can be understood only of the 'souls' coming out of Sheol, to which they had descended like the 'souls' of the sinners." But we have just seen that this is impossible.

3

The Book of Wisdom

The author of Wisdom identifies himself as King Solomon (9:7-8, 12), but this is in virtue of a literary fiction that deceived no one (See Prov 1:1; 10:1; 25:1; Eccl 1:1, 12; Cant 1:1). In reality, the book was written in Greek toward the end of the first century B.C.E.[24] by an educated Jew living in Alexandria, the great Mediterranean port where Jews and Greeks lived side by side. It is usual to distinguish three parts in the book; for instance, here is the division proposed by Chrysostome Larcher:[25] 1. The human condition is discussed in the light of the different destinies of the just and the wicked (1:1-5:23). 2. Divine Wisdom comes to the aid of people to help them reach their goal (6:1-11:1). 3. The special history of a holy people, battling idolatrous adversaries, illustrates the different fates reserved for the righteous and the evildoers and sheds light on some aspects of divine providence (11:2-19:22).

---

[24] See Gilbert, "Sagesse," cols. 91-92: "The present tendency is to bring Wisdom's date of composition forward to the second half of the first century B.C.E. . . . and more precisely after 30 B.C.E. or even . . . at the time of Christ or a few decades prior to it." According to Larcher, *Sagesse*, 161, the definitive redaction would have to be pushed forward to about 15 or 10 B.C.E.

[25] Larcher, *Sagesse*, 120-123.

But there is a problem of some concern to us, that of the literary composition of the book.[26] It is often more acutely felt on this particular point: Were the first two parts, on the one hand, and the third, on the other, written by the same author? Certain commentators have drawn attention to the considerable thematic and stylistic differences between the first two parts and the third, and they have concluded that two different authors were involved in the composition of the book. Those who were convinced of the unity of the book replied by stressing the undeniable uniformity of style throughout the book. We cannot go into the discussion of this problem. However, it seems to us that we must admit, *at the least,* Larcher's position: "At the end of these efforts to identify more precisely the addressees of the book, it is already clear that it was not composed all at the same time and in the same historical context; we must suppose a certain interval between the main sections" (p. 118). The author, according to Larcher, took care of the definitive edition of the book and at that time would have made some changes: "Finally [the author] must have put the last touches on his book by strengthening the necessary transitions, adding some complements, even perhaps introducing numerical or harmonic correspondences" (p. 119). Let us also note what Larcher writes concerning the third part of the work in which some sections seem weakly linked to their context, "Because the whole book nonetheless bears the stamp of one and the same literary personality, the author must have taken up, reworked, and harmonized themes that had been treated before by him *or by others.*[27] As a consequence, certain traits may belong to a previous period"[28] (p. 161).

---

[26] See the exposition of this complex problem in Larcher, *Sagesse,* 95–119.

[27] Our emphasis.

[28] It is the position which we shall adopt later on. However, see Gilbert's reservations in "Sagesse," col. 93: "That the book was not written in a day is obvious; but it seems to us to evidence more unity than C. Larcher thought."

We shall come back to this problem of the composition of Wisdom when we need to do so. But right now, we shall illustrate it by an example which can serve as an introduction to the topic of the present book. This is not mentioned by Larcher when he reviews the arguments advanced by those who contest that chapters 1–9 on the one hand and 10–19 on the other are the work of the same writer (pp. 98–100).

Two Different Anthropologies

a) *Semitic anthropology*. In Wisdom 15:7-19, the author upbraids those who fashion idols out of clay extracted from the earth. Several verses clearly show that in this passage he follows a Semitic anthropology based on the account of the creation of human beings in Genesis 2:7. Here is the text according to the Septuagint:[29]

> And God formed [*eplasen*] the human, dust [drawn] from the earth [*choun apo tēs gēs*] and breathed [*enephsēsen*] on its face a breath of life [*pnoēn zōēs*] and the human became a living being [*psuchēn zōsan*].

Now let us see what the author of Wisdom has against the idol maker in 15:11, quoted according to the New Jerusalem Bible:

> For he has misconceived the One who has modelled [*ton plasanta*] him,
> who breathed an active soul [*psuchēn*] into him,
> and inspired [*emphusēsanta*] a living spirit [*pneuma zōtikon*].

In Greek, the word *psuchē* first means "breath," then, more precisely, "breath of life," hence "soul" as the principle of life.[30] Therefore, it is clear that we have here an echo of the sentence in Genesis 2:7, "[God] breathed on its face a breath of life" (LXX). As a note to Wisdom 15:11 in the Bible de

---

[29] We already analyzed this passage when we spoke of 1 Cor 15:45 (pp. 42–43).

[30] See Liddell–Scott, *Lexicon*.

Jérusalem accurately says, "'Active soul' and 'breath of life' are synonymous." So it is obvious that in this passage the author of Wisdom does not take the word "soul" in its philosophical sense, that is, as opposed to the body, but identifies it with the impersonal vital breath of which Genesis 2:7 speaks.

This is confirmed for us by verse 8 of the same chapter where it is said about the idol maker, according to the New Jerusalem Bible:

> Then—ill-spent effort!—from the same clay he models [*plassei*] a futile god,
> although so recently made out of earth himself
> and shortly to return to what he was taken from,
> when asked to give back the soul [*psuchē*] that has been lent to him.

We shall note in passing the allusion to Genesis 3:19, where God announces their punishment to rebellious humans, "until you return to the ground, for out of it you were taken." Besides, at death, God takes back the souls *lent* to humans when God created them. The same idea is found in Ecclesiastes 12:7, "The dust returns to the earth as it was, and the breath returns to God who gave it."

Let us also read Wisdom 15:16:

> For a human being made them,
> and one whose spirit is borrowed [*to pneuma dedaneismenos*] formed them. . . .

This verse confirms the fundamental identity between the two terms *pneuma* and *psuchē;* both designate the vital breath lent by God to humans and by God withdrawn at the moment of death. As in Genesis 2:7, it is the "breath" that gives life; when God takes it back, humans cease living, they die.

However, there is a text in 16:13-14 which supplies us with an important clarification:

> 13. For you have power over life and death,
> you lead mortals down to the gates of Hades and back again.
> 14. A person in wickedness kills another,

> but cannot bring back the departed spirit[[*pneuma*],
> or set free the imprisoned soul [*psuchē*].

As in the preceding texts, *pneuma* and *psuchē* designate the vital breath. As what is said in verse 13 shows, after coming out of a person, the *psuchē* of verse 14 was received in Hades, or Sheol as the Bible de Jérusalem interprets it in a note. It is difficult to reconcile this text with that of 15:8 where it is said that the *psuchē* is simply lent to humans and that humans return to the earth from which they were taken when God takes it back. Be that as it may, we are still within a purely Semitic outlook.

b) *A Platonic anthropology.* We must now analyze some texts from the first two parts of the book of Wisdom. They present us with a resolutely Platonic view. The first text is 9:15, which we shall give first in the Greek, then in English translation:

> *phtarton gar sōma barunei psuchēn*
> *kai brithei to geōdēs skēnos noun poluphrontida.*

> for a perishable body weighs down the soul,
> and this earthly tent burdens the thoughtful mind.

Let us compare this to what Plato wrote in the *Phaedo* (81):

> *embrithes de ge . . . touto oiesthai chrē einai kai baru kai*
> *geōdēs kai horaton . . . ho dē kai echonta hē toiautē psuchē*
> *barunetai.*

> And this corporeal element . . . is heavy and weighty and earthy, and is that element of sight by which a soul is depressed and dragged down. . . .

The idea is the same, expressed in words rather rare in Greek and in part identical (verb and adjective): the soul is distinct from the body, which, drawn from the earth and corruptible, weighs heavy on the soul and hinders the full functioning of intelligence.[31] Although it is not explicitly said, it

---

[31] See Larcher, *Sagesse,* 210: "The language is clearly Platonic."

is clear that the soul, opposed to the body, is incorruptible and therefore immortal. The theme of the body likened to a tent is also Platonic.

Another text, Wisdom 8:19-20, is equally telling, "As a child I was naturally gifted, / and a good soul fell to my lot; / or rather, being good, I entered an undefiled body." Larcher comments, "The *Timaeus* 34 and 36 would directly elucidate Wisdom 8:19-20: the soul is the real self and the spirit comes into existence before matter" (p. 210). Here in Wisdom 8:20, we would be in the presence of the Platonic theme of the soul's existing before coming to inhabit an earthy body.[32] However, the author's hesitation should be noted: it is as though he alluded to the Platonic theme only on second thought.

Finally, let us see how, in 2:2-4, the author describes the idea sinners have of their destiny after death:

> 2. For we were born by mere chance,
> and hereafter we shall be as though we had never been,
> for the breath [*pnoē*] in our nostrils is smoke [*kapnos*],
> and reason is a spark kindled by the beating of our hearts;
> 3. when it is extinguished, the body will turn to ashes,
> and the spirit will dissolve like empty air.
> 4.   · · · · ·
> our life will pass away like [*hōs*] the traces of a cloud, and
> be scattered [*diaskedasthèsetai*] like mist
> that is chased by the rays of the sun.

Here again, we rejoin Plato (*Phaedo* 70) depicting how those who do not accept that the soul is immortal imagine the afterlife:

> [The soul] may be nowhere, and . . . on the very day of death she may perish and come to an end–immediately on her release from the body, issuing forth dispersed like [*hōsper*] smoke [*kapnos*] or air and in her flight vanishing away [*diaskedastheisa*] into nothingness.

Among all these texts, the most important is incontestably Wisdom 9:15: it demonstrates most clearly that in

---

[32] Many commentators interpret this text in different ways.

the first two parts of the book, the author has resolutely adopted a Platonic anthropology.[33] Our further analysis will confirm it. However, it would be imprudent to conclude that chapters 10–19 are the work of an author other than the one of chapters 1–9. For instance, in 15:3 we read, "For to know you is complete righteousness, / and to know your power is the root of immortality." This notion of immortality, which will be found again in some texts from the first part of the book, is without any doubt Greek, not Semitic, and immediately precedes the development of 15:7-19, which exhibits a Semitic anthropology. The problem of the literary unity of the work is therefore a complex one. Further on, we shall observe more of this complexity.

The Final Destiny of the Righteous

We may now ask ourselves how the author of Wisdom envisages the final destiny of the righteous. It is a decidedly Platonic approach:[34] at the end of their earthly lives, human beings continue to live thanks to their souls, which are immortal. Nevertheless, we must answer an essential question: Upon leaving the body, does the soul go directly to the world of the divine, as Plato thinks, or must it not first pass through Sheol (Hades) where it has to wait for the time when it will be able to join God in heaven, as in the book of Enoch?

a) In 4:7-14, the writer treats the case of the just who die prematurely: Was it not a scandal for many (v. 15)? Was not God bound to maintain in life for a long time, and in prosperous conditions, those who faithfully observed the divine

---

[33] Nevertheless, it must be noted that in 1:6, the loins and the heart seem to be the seat of the passions, in accordance with the usual way of speaking in the Old Testament.

[34] Our conclusions coincide for a large part with Grelot, "L'eschatologie." However, we diverge from him as to the idea of the soul going down to Sheol after death. We are speaking of the soul as Plato thought of it, not of the *nefesh* of Semetic thought, which God lent to humans and which God takes away at the moment of death (Wis 15:8, 11, 16).

law? The author reveals his key thought in verse 10, quoted according to the New Jerusalem Bible, "Having won God's favor [*euarestos*], he has been loved / and, as he was living among sinners, has been taken away [*metetethē*]." The beginning and the end of the verse refer to the text of Genesis 5:24 according to the Septuagint, which speaks of Enoch at the end of his life on earth, "Enoch walked with God [was pleasing *(euērestēsen)* to God]; then he was no more, because God took him [*metethēken*]" (see also Sir 44:16; Heb 11:5). The just who die prematurely have the same fate as Enoch: they leave earth without dying. This obviously rests on the supposition that their souls go to another place. This would be explicitly stated in verse 14 if this possible translation was adopted, "The soul of the just was pleasing [*arestē*] to God, so it came out in haste from the midst of perversity."[35] Whatever the case with this last text, since the author of the book has adopted, as we have seen, a Platonic anthropology, he certainly thinks that it is the soul of the just that has been taken.

However, Wisdom does not tell us where the soul goes. In verse 7, we learn only that it finds rest. If the author thought that the soul goes directly to God, would the text not tell us in clear terms? Our following analysis will show that this silence effectively reveals that on this point, the writer had modified the Platonic conception.

b) But let us turn to the pivotal text, 2:21–3:9. Nickelsburg[36] has aptly demonstrated that it is part of a long section divided into two parts, an excellent parallel to which is found in Enoch 102–103. In their first parts, both books reveal what the impious think: this life is short (Wis 2:1-5; Enoch 102:6-8); therefore, we must enjoy it (Wis 2:6-9; Enoch 102:9a) while oppressing the righteous (Wis 2:10-16; Enoch 102:9b), who are without hope of rescue (Wis 2:18-20;

---

[35] The Greek text does not reveal whether the subject of the verb is masculine or feminine.

[36] Nickelsburg, *Resurrection*, 129. On the relationship between Wisdom and Enoch 91–104, see Larcher, *Etudes*, 106–112.

Enoch 102:10-11). In their second parts, this reasoning is refuted: it is necessary to know God's mystery (mysteries) (Wis 2:21-24; Enoch 103:1-2), that is, to know that the souls of the just will be protected by God (Wis 3:1-9; Enoch 103:3-4) while sinners will be punished (Wis 3:10-12; Enoch 103:5-8); there follows an "anti-deuterocanonical" section (Wis 3:13–4:9; Enoch 103:9-15). Let us examine whether the final destiny of the righteous is conceived in the same way in both Wisdom and Enoch.

– In Wisdom 2:16b-20, the evildoers deride the just, who have asserted that since they live in accordance with the divine law, God is bound to protect them by snatching them from the hands of their enemies. Let us put the just to death and this will be the proof that they were in error: God did not protect them.

But these critics are badly mistaken because they are ignorant of the "mysteries of God" (2:21-22a). They do not want to believe that despite appearances, God rewards *pure souls* (2:22b). Indeed, God created humans for incorruptibility *(ep' aphtharsia)*, made them in the image of God's own nature (v. 23; cf. Gen 1:26). The author's readers must already have understood that at death, even if the body, the visible part of the human being, disappears and decays in the ground, humans continue to live thanks to their souls, which were created in God's likeness and are therefore incorruptible. This is the theme, developed in 3:1-9, we must now explain verse by verse.

– "But the souls of the righteous are in the hand of God, / and no torment [*basanos*] will ever touch them" (3:1). This verse is a response to the sarcasm of the wicked, "Let us test him with insult and torture [*basanoi*]" (2:19). Although they were put to death, the just cannot now be affected by the torments inflicted by the evildoers. Their souls are "in the hand of God"; this does not mean that they are already with God, but only that they are protected by God (cf. Deut 33:3; John 10:28-29).

– "In the eyes of the foolish they seemed to have died, / and their departure was thought to be a disaster, / and their going from us to be their destruction; / but they are in peace"

(3:2-3). The author of the book continues to answer the sarcasm of the impious, "Let us condemn him to a shameful death, / for, according to what he says, he will be protected" (2:20). Contrary to what the foolish think, death is only an appearance since the soul lives on (see 4 Macc 13:14[37]). Humans are not reduced to nothing, but through their souls go into another place, as if setting out on a journey. We find again the theme of the just who die prematurely: they have been "transferred" (4:10; cf. Gen 5:24). The writer does not tell us yet where they are transported but only says that they are "in peace," they are no longer at the mercy of the sinners' persecution, as was already said in verse 1. We must admit that the author is very slow in telling us that the souls of the just are *now* in God. If this was the thought, why was it not said in clear terms?

– "For though in the sight of others they were punished, / their hope is full of immortality [*aphtharsia*]" (3:4). We are still dealing with the paradox of the destiny of the just and the contrast between what appears "in the sight of others" and what happens in reality. Physical death is only an appearance (v. 2a) since human beings, thanks to their souls, are immortal; they cannot die.

– "Having been disciplined a little, / they will receive great good, / because God tested them and found them worthy of himself; / like gold in the furnace he tried them, / and like a sacrificial burnt offering he accepted them" (3:5-6). Death and the sufferings that precede it must be regarded as trials sent by God to test the faithfulness of the just, as the quality of gold is ascertained in the fire of the crucible (cf. Gen 22:1; Tob 12:14; Job 1:12; Ps 66:10).

– "In the time of their visitation they will shine forth [*analampsousin*]" (3:7a). This is the same verb as in Enoch 104:2 [*analēmpsetai*]. One notes that the future tense is used here in contrast to the present tense found in verses 1 and 3. The Bible de Jérusalem in a note to this verse aptly comments on the words "in the time of their visitation": "The expression itself . . . implies a later phase in the condition of upright

---

[37] See part 2, ch. 5 (p. 97), devoted to 4 Maccabees.

souls. The verb which follows presumably means their final glorification." Let us attempt to see more clearly what this "visitation" is. The Greek noun *episkopē* derives from the verb *episkopein* which means "to examine, to look at attentively, to scrutinize." In Wisdom 1:6, God is called the *episkopos* of the human heart, the one who examines it to see whether it be good or bad. This probing action entails a divine intervention, a punishment for the sinners (cf. Isa 10:3; Jer 6:15; 10:15), but on the contrary, a beneficial, often salvific action for the righteous. Thus, in Genesis 50:24-25 (LXX), Joseph tells his brothers, "I am about to die, but God will surely visit [*episkopēi episkepsetai*] you, and bring you up out of this land to the land that he swore to Abraham, to Isaac, and to Jacob." And Job in 10:12 (LXX) states, "Your visitation has preserved my spirit," in the sense that God has saved him from death. In the book of Wisdom, the visitation of God *always* has a favorable meaning. The impious railed against the just by saying, "Let us condemn him to a shameful death, / for, according to what he says, there will be a visitation for him." The object of this "visitation" is not to save the just one from physical death, but to save him after his death (3:7, 9; cf. 4:15). It seems that at the time it occurs, this visitation will have a collective dimension and will extend to all the just at once. "Blessed the sterile woman if she be blameless . . . for she will have fruit at the visitation of souls" (3:13; NJB).

Although it is not explicitly said, it is possible to be more precise and think that the visitation of God in favor of the righteous will consist in having them come up from Hades (Sheol). Indeed, in 2:1, the impious erroneously imagine, "No one has been known to return [*ho analusas*] from Hades." It is true that human beings "cannot bring back the departed spirit or set free the imprisoned soul" (16:14), but God can: "For you have power over life and death; / you lead mortals down to the gates of Hades and back again [*anageis*]" (16:13). The thought is identical with that expressed in the book of Enoch: at death, the souls of the just leave their bodies in order to go down to Hades, where they will remain until the time of the visitation; then God will bring them out all together from this place of waiting and "they will shine forth" (Wis 3:7a).

– In the book of Enoch, the souls of the righteous will shine forth in heaven, whose doors are open for them (104:2). Here, in Wisdom 3:9, we learn that at the time of the visitation, "the faithful will abide with him in love." And in 6:19, we even read that incorruptibility causes the righteous to be near God. In 5:15-16a, the final destiny is described in these words, "But the righteous live forever, / and their reward [cf. 2:22c] is with the Lord; / the Most High takes care of them. / Therefore they will receive a glorious crown / and a beautiful diadem from the hand of the Lord." In 5:5, on the day of judgment, the evildoers, who have remained in Hades, will ask themselves concerning the just they had persecuted and mocked in the past, "Why have they been numbered among the children of God? / And why is their lot among the saints?" There has been much discussion about who "God's children" and "the saints" are. We adopt Larcher's opinion,[38] shared by many other writers, according to which these terms would apply to angels, who frequently are called thus in the Bible. Once more, we discover that here there is a parallel with the book of Enoch, which says that the just go to join the angels in heaven (104:4). On the day of God's visitation, the souls of the just will be freed from Hades and led to heaven to dwell with God forever.

The Fate of the Wicked

The impious will remain in death because this is their wish. They call for death with deeds and words, they consider it their friend, they form an alliance with it; therefore, they deserve to belong to it (1:16; cf. 2:24). How are we to understand these words? The dead seem to be assembled in one place. Indeed, it is said of them, "After this they will become dishonored corpses, / and an outrage among the dead forever" (4:18). In 1:14, Hades is a personification of death. We must therefore deduce that the sinners will be gathered in Hades, from which they will never come out.

[38] Larcher, *Sagesse*, 364.

It is there that they will be judged[39] by God when "their sins are reckoned up, / and their lawless deeds will convict them to their face" (4:20). They will then realize they were wrong to harass the just with sarcasm (5:2-5; cf. 2:10-20); they can now see that the righteous are numbered among the children of God (cf. 2:18) and the saints (5:5); they can fathom the emptiness of their past life (5:6-14).

Contrary to Enoch, Wisdom does not speak of the terrible suffering of the sinners. Their punishment lies in the fact that they can never leave Hades and enjoy God's presence.

Platonism and Judaism

The preceding analysis enables us to formulate the following conclusions. In chapters 1–9, when envisaging the final destiny of humanity, the author of Wisdom strives to establish a compromise between Platonic and Jewish thought. It is not a new position since all the writer does is repeat what the book of Enoch has said in chapters 102–104. Following Plato, the author accepts that the human person is made up of a soul, the seat of personality, and a body. At the end of this earthly life, the soul abandons the body; but whereas the body disintegrates in the earth from which it was taken, the soul lives on because it is incorruptible and immortal.[40] Finally, the souls of the just are called to enjoy a blessed eternity with God.

However, and it is on this point that the author of Wisdom parts company with Platonism, the souls of the just do not immediately join God. They begin by descending into Hades, exactly like the souls of the evildoers, and it is only at the time of the visitation that they will leave Hades in order to go and live with God. The Jewish theme of the descent into Sheol after death is enunciated here, but with an essential difference. In the Semitic concept, which did not distin-

---

[39] The BJ rightly observes in a note to 4:20–5:14, the final judgment, "This judgment, however, concerns only the godless, since the upright have already been admitted to the presence of God; cf. 5:4-5."

[40] Probably in virtue of a gift from God and not by nature, as Plato thought.

guish the soul from the body, the dead remained in Sheol like emaciated shades whose form of life was diminished to the extreme. In contrast, the author of the book of Wisdom thinks that the human soul which goes down to Sheol keeps its entire personality, its complete psychic life.

A Resurrection of the Body?

Some authors have thought that although Wisdom does not explicitly speak of it, the writer implicitly accepted that there is a resurrection of the body. But we think this hypothesis is excluded for the following reason: according to Platonic theory, a resurrection of the body was unthinkable. Why would the author of Wisdom have admitted such a resurrection since for both the author and Plato, the body is an obstacle to the full exercise of the soul's intellectual faculties (Wis 9:15)? To maintain that the author of Wisdom envisaged a resurrection of the body, one would have to offer very serious arguments. Let us examine those that have been proposed.

The main argument relies on the text of Wisdom 5:16b-23, a passage showing God going to war against the enemies of God's people in order to exterminate them. This would suppose, the argument goes, that the just and the evildoers still live in their bodies. But let us take a closer look. In fact, we have here a traditional biblical theme. The pseudo-historical context is given at the end, in 23b, "Lawlessness will lay waste the whole earth, / and evil-doing will overturn the thrones of rulers." But God comes to the aid of the faithful by putting on a warrior's armor (vv. 16b-20a). The whole cosmos takes up arms to help God in this battle: flashes of lightning, hailstones, billows of the sea, overflowing rivers, tempestuous wind join forces to destroy the wicked (vv. 20b-23a). The whole passage is composed of biblical reminiscences, especially Isaiah 59:17, describing God's avenging action against the impious.[41] There are also striking parallels to God's action against the Egyptians as depicted in the third

---

[41] For details, readers may consult the notes and marginal references of the NJB or BJ.

part of Exodus. We read in Wisdom 5:17b, "[The Lord] will arm all creation [*ktisis*] to repel his enemies," as in 16:24, "For creation [*ktisis*] . . . exerts itself to punish the unrighteous." One can also establish a comparison with 5:20, "and creation [*kosmos*] will join with him to fight against his frenzied foes," and with 16:17, "for the universe [*kosmos*] defends the righteous." The closest parallelism is found between 5:23a, "A mighty wind [*pneuma dunameōs*] will rise against them, and like a tempest will winnow [*eklimēsei*] them away," and 11:20, "and scattered by the breath of your power [*likmēthentes hupo pneumatos dunameōs sou*]." One understands that the impious will be destroyed and that God's people will be able to live in peace on earth. This is one of the classical themes of the Jewish apocalyptic tradition.

But who does not see that this extravagantly eloquent passage is out of place here? The just have already obtained their reward with God (5:15). After having sheltered them in Hades, where they are beyond the reach of the torments inflicted by sinners (2:22; 3:1), where they enjoy peace (3:3), God has given them a place near God on the day of their visitation (3:7a, 9). And could they be the same just who receive "the beautiful diadem" and "the glorious crown" (5:16a) "because [*hoti*]" God will exterminate their enemies *on earth* (5:16b-23)? The Bible de Jérusalem has clearly seen the difficulty since it comments in a note on verse 15, "This section is perhaps alluding to a specific eschatological event." In order to preserve a certain logic to this passage, this note should refer to verse 16b rather than 15. But how shall we understand this "eschatological event"? Is it a matter of "catastrophes unleashed for the final punishment of the wicked," as the Bible de Jérusalem says in the same note? Certainly not, since on the day of judgment, the souls of the unrighteous will be in Hades and not on earth as our present text supposes. In any case, this event does not concern the just since, to say it once more, they are already near God. This passage cannot prove that the author of Wisdom believed in the resurrection of the body!

It is therefore the whole problem of the composition of Wisdom which is the difficulty. We have here, inserted after 5:16a, a piece belonging to an altogether different context which repeats the traditional Jewish idea of a destruction of the persecuting sinners while they are still on earth.

We have a similar problem in 3:7-9. Verses 7a and 9 describe the final destiny of the souls of the just once God will have visited them and frame verses 7b-8, "[They] will run like sparks through the stubble. / They will govern nations and rule over peoples, / and the Lord will reign over them forever." This is a classical apocalyptic theme, similar to the one we saw in 5:16b-23: the nations that oppose God's people *on earth* will be destroyed and the reign of God will be established in peace (cf. Isa 1:31; 5:24; Nah 1:10; Obad 18). All this can happen only *before* the day of visitation and in no way concerns the destiny of the souls of the just. One needs a great deal of imagination to see in this short passage proof that the author of Wisdom conceived of a resurrection of the body. Like 5:16b-23, we have here an erratic fragment inserted into the text of Wisdom at a later date, at the time of the final redaction of the book.[42]

Psalms 49 and 73

The explanation we have given on the books of Enoch and Wisdom enable us to understand two difficult passages in Psalms 49 and 73. The similarities between them and Enoch and Wisdom are evident.[43] The general context is that of the just who, on earth, are tempted and do not understand why the evildoers enjoy prosperity while they themselves are persecuted by them (Ps 49:6-7, 17-18; Ps 73:2-12; see especially Enoch 102:4-11). But the psalmist finally understands God's plan. The impious are condemned to remain forever in Sheol:

> Like sheep they are appointed for Sheol;
>   Death shall be their shepherd;
> straight to the grave they descend,
>   and their form shall waste away;
>   Sheol shall be their home (Ps 49:14; cf. Ps 73:18-19).

---

[42] We do not think that these interpolations are due to the author of Wisdom.

[43] See Barucq, "O salmo 49."

On the contrary, the final destiny of the just is to be with God:

> But God will ransom my soul from the power of Sheol,
>> for he will receive me (Ps 49:15).

> Nevertheless I am continually with you;
>> you hold my right hand.
> You guide me with your counsel,
>> and afterward you will receive me with honor (Ps 73:23-24).

We have seen that Wisdom 4:10 compared the fate of the just one who dies prematurely with that of the patriarch Enoch transferred from one place to another (LXX Gen 5:24). Both Psalms 49 and 73 say that the just will not remain in Sheol because God will "take" them up. It is the same Hebrew verb as that used to describe Enoch's fate in Genesis 5:24. We think that Grelot[44] is right in seeing in both psalms, as in the book of Wisdom, an echo of the text of Genesis 5:24. Thus, we seem to have the same scenario as in Enoch and Wisdom: at death, all souls go down to Sheol, those of the just as well as those of the evildoers. But a day will come when God will "take up" the souls of the just to free them from Sheol and lead them into divine glory, whereas the souls of the wicked will remain in the abode of the dead.[45]

An Echo in the New Testament

This theme can explain a difficult text in 1 Peter 3:18-19, probably an ancient hymn quoted by the author:

> For Christ also suffered for sins once for all,
>> the righteous for the unrighteous
>>> in order to bring you to God.

---

[44] Grelot, "La légende," 210.

[45] Puech, *La croyance,* 52, even thinks that the text of Ps 49:15—of which he gives a translation quite different from that of the BJ—explicitly affirms that in Sheol, the just and the wicked will be separated. In this case, Ps 49 would be even closer to what is stated in Enoch.

> He was put to death in the flesh,
>> but made alive in the spirit,
>>> in which also he went and made a proclamation to the
>>> spirits in prison.

This early hymn supposes a real distinction between the soul and the body (the flesh) since Christ, put to death as to the flesh, remained alive in his spirit. It is with his spirit that he went to preach to the "spirits in prison." Commentators agree that the "prison" is Hades.[46] The spirits (the souls) of the just await their final liberation when God will bring them out of Sheol to keep them close (v. 18). Therefore, Christ went down to Hades to announce to the spirits of the just that the time was near when they would come out to go with God. To repeat the expression of the book of Wisdom, "the time of their visitation" is at hand.[47]

---

[46] Some Greek manuscripts have changed "prison" to "Hades."

[47] See also perhaps Rev 6:9: the souls of the martyrs are assembled under the altar of the Temple. They are told to wait a little longer.

————— 4 —————

The Second Letter of Paul to the Corinthians

— (Chs. 3 and 5) —

Now we are going to analyze Paul's teaching in 2 Corinthians 3 and 5 concerning the individual's final fate. We shall see that Paul also blends Platonic theory and Jewish thought, but in a different way. Abandoning Semitic anthropology, he adopts a Platonic anthropology which will lead him to conceive of our individual end differently from what he had explained in 1 Corinthians. Perhaps this move was a tactical one since his preaching is more and more frequently addressed to Greek-educated pagans and less and less to Jews (see Gal 2:8; Acts 13:46). He knows from experience that the Greeks are allergic to any notion of resurrection (see Acts 17:31-32). So he adopts the theme of immortality and leaves aside that of resurrection. However, far from being tactical only, this change, as we shall see, is chiefly due to a profound theological reason.

In order to conduct our study well, let us compare a few verses from 2 Corinthians 3 and 5 with certain verses from 1 Corinthians 15 which we have analyzed in a previous chapter:[48]

_____

[48] For the Greek word *pneuma* (which means "breath" or "spirit"), see part 1, ch. 5, pp. 42–45.

1 Cor 15	*2 Cor 3*
it is raised in glory (v. 43) it is raised a spiritual [*pneumatikon*] body (v. 44) the last Adam (Christ)	the ministry of the Spirit [*pneuma*] come[s] in glory (v. 8) Now the Lord is the Spirit [*pneuma*] (v. 17)
became a life-giving spirit [*pneuma*] (v. 45)	but the Spirit [*pneuma*] gives life (v. 6) seeing the glory of the Lord [in] the same image
we will also bear the image of the man of heaven (v. 49) and we will be changed (v. 52)	[we] are being transformed from one degree of glory to another (v. 18)
	2 Cor 5
[opposition between earthly beings and heavenly beings (vv. 40, 47, 49)]	[opposition between our earthly dwelling and our heavenly dwelling (v. 1)]
this mortal body must put on immortality (v. 53)	For we groan, longing to be clothed with our heavenly dwelling (v. 2)
When . . . this mortal body puts on immortality, then the saying that is written will be fulfilled: Death has been swallowed up in victory (v. 54)	For . . . we groan . . . because we wish not to be unclothed, but to be further clothed so that what is mortal may be swallowed up by life (v. 4)

The parallelism between the two series of texts is obvious. But the perspective of 2 Corinthians 3 and 5 is very different from that of 1 Corinthians 15.

A Realized Eschatology

We shall begin by studying the text of 2 Corinthians 3:17-18 which will give us the necessary key for entering into Paul's thought.

a) In order to understand this text, we must take into account the previous context. Verses 4-11 are dominated by the theme of "glory" since this noun appears eight times and the verb "to be glorified" appears twice. Let us recall that in 1 Corinthians 15, "glory" was the privilege of risen beings (vv. 40-43). Here, Paul wants to show the supereminence of the New Covenant and he reasons as follows. His point of departure is the scene recorded in Exodus 34:29-35: when Moses spoke with God on Sinai, the skin of his face became glorious, that is, illuminated by the divine glory it reflected. But Moses was the minister of a covenant based on the letter (the Tables of the Law) and the letter kills; the ministry of the New Covenant, on the contrary, is based on the Spirit, which gives life (3:6). The conclusion is inescapable: "Now if the ministry of death, chiseled in letters on stone tablets, came in [such] glory . . . how much more will the ministry of the Spirit come in glory?" (3:7-8) and also "For if there was glory in the ministry of condemnation, much more does the ministry of justification abound in glory!" (3:9). One thing is sure, divine glory is superabundant in the New Covenant.

The text continues by elaborating on the fact reported in Exodus 34:33-35: when Moses had finished speaking with God, he put a veil on his face; and Paul comments, "so that the Israelites should not watch the end of what was transitory" (v. 13; NJB). In other words, the Israelites could not understand the meaning of the Old Covenant. Similarly, Paul adds, even today, a veil remains on the hearts of the Jews[49] since they do not understand the Law when they read it. It is Christ who removes the veil, who gives their correct meaning to the narratives of the Old Testament; it is therefore when one turns to the Lord (Christ) that the veil is lifted and one understands the true meaning of the Scriptures (vv. 14-16).

---

[49] As he often does elsewhere, Paul slides from one theme to the other; here, from the theme of the "veil over Moses's face" to that of the "veil over the Jews' faces."

b) We now come to the crucial text of verses 17-18.

> Now this Lord is the Spirit [*pneuma*] and where the Spirit [*pneuma*] of the Lord is, there is freedom. And all of us, with our unveiled faces like mirrors reflecting the glory of the Lord, are being transformed into the image that we reflect in brighter and brighter glory; this is the working of the Lord who is the Spirit [*pneuma*] (NJB).

First, let us give a few words of explanation on the translation of this difficult text. In the beginning of verse 17, the title "Lord" certainly applies to Christ, not to the God of the Old Testament, as some commentators have thought with the praiseworthy intention of avoiding a difficulty: Paul's identification of Christ and the Spirit. Indeed, the preceding verse says that "when one turns to the Lord, the veil is removed." But what the Jews—this passage is about them—needed in Paul's view was to be converted to Christ, to recognize him as sent by God, not to be converted to the true God, which they did not need to do.[50] Besides, it is clear that the "Lord" mentioned in verses 16-17 is identical with Christ, named in verse 14. Lastly, the parallelism between this text and that of 1 Corinthians 15:45, highlighted above, shows clearly that Christ is the life-giving *pneuma*. In verse 18, the Greek verb *katoptrizesthai* may mean "to reflect as in a mirror" or "to contemplate as in a mirror." The first meaning is the obvious one because of the preceding verses (7-15): there is a contrast between Moses, who veiled his face so that the glory that shone from it would not be seen, and us, Christians who with unveiled faces reflect the glory of the Lord, that is, the glory of Christ. By reflecting this glory, "we are being transformed into the same image." The glorious Christ is God's image (2 Cor 4:4; cf. Col 1:15); by reflecting his glory, we are also transformed into the image of the divine glory.

c) In order to understand the evolution of Paul's thought, let us recall what we explained about 1 Corinthians 15:45-54. At the end of time, at his return, Christ will play the role of the

---

[50] If the pagans were the ones the text means, there would be a need to be converted to the true God.

life-giving *pneuma* of which Genesis 2:7 speaks. He will effect as it were a new creation. Through him, the dead will rise, imbued with divine glory, and all those still alive at the time will be transformed by putting on the incorruptibility given by glory, that is, immortality, and death will be destroyed. Here also, Christ is the *pneuma* (2 Cor 3:17), and the life-giving *pneuma* (2 Cor 3:6), the principle of a new creation. But it is right now that we "are being transformed into the image that we reflect in brighter and brighter glory" by the Lord who is *pneuma*. Paul has gone from classical eschatology to what is called nowadays "realized eschatology." According to 1 Corinthians, we were to "put on" immortality at the time of Christ's return. But Paul has now understood that at baptism, we have "been clothed" with Christ: "As many of you as were baptized into Christ have clothed yourselves with Christ" (Gal 3:27; cf. Rom 13:14). Along the same lines, Paul (or one of his disciples) writes to the faithful at Ephesus, "You were taught to put away your former way of life, your old self, corrupt [*ton phtheiromenon*] and deluded by its lusts, and to be renewed in the spirit of your minds, and to clothe [*endusasthai*] yourselves with the new self, created [*ktisthenta*] according to the likeness of God in true righteousness and holiness" (4:22-24). Finally, a little farther on in 2 Corinthians, Paul writes, "So if anyone is in Christ, there is a new creation: everything old has passed away; see, everything has become new! All this is from God . . ." (5:17-18). In 1 Corinthians 15:45-54, it was only at the time of his return that Christ, life-giving *pneuma* (Gen 2:7), was the principle of a new creation, in God's glory; but now, Paul has understood that because we put on Christ at baptism, the new creation is already here.

An extremely important consequence flows from this new way of seeing things. Since we possess within us Christ, life-giving *pneuma*, we have already risen. Later on, Paul will say:

> When you were buried with him in baptism, you were also raised with him through faith in the power of God, who raised him from the dead. And when you were dead in trespasses and the uncircumcision of your flesh, God made you alive together with him, when he forgave us all our trespasses (Col 2:12-13; cf. Rom 6:2-4).

But at some point in the future, one of Paul's disciples will be scandalized because two Christians, Hymenaeus and Philetus, contend that "the resurrection has already taken place" (2 Tim 2:18). By any chance would it be that these two were the ones who had truly understood Paul's thought?

Another consequence is ineluctable. We have seen that in 1 Corinthians 15, Paul had kept the schemes of early Semitic anthropology, which made no distinction between soul and body. But Paul finds it impossible to continue to adhere to such an anthropology. For if we now already possess in ourselves Christ, life-giving *pneuma,* principle of resurrection, this resurrection can affect only our souls since our bodies will decay in the earth. Only a Platonic anthropology can account for our present resurrection. Since our body will one day disintegrate, it is necessary for us to have a soul, distinct from it, which will never die because at baptism it has put on Christ, life-giving *pneuma.* Effectively, this is what we shall see to be the case when we proceed to explain 2 Corinthians 5:1-10.

A Platonic Anthropology

According to the schemes of Semitic anthropology, which did not distinguish the soul from the body, when human beings die, they descend into Sheol as unsubstantial shades, perhaps even completely disappear into the ground from which they were taken (Gen 3:19). They no longer have any personality. The analysis of 2 Corinthians 5:1-10 will show that Paul completely abandoned this understanding in order to adopt another one akin to Platonic views, but with an important modification concerning the body. For clarity's sake, we first will explain the text of 5:6-8:

> 6. So we are always confident; even though we know that while we are at home [*endēmountes*] in the body we are away [*ekdēmoumen*] from the Lord—
> 7. for we walk by faith, not by sight.
> 8. Yes, we do have confidence, and we would rather be away [*ekdēmēsai*] from the body and at home [*endēmēsai*] with the Lord.

Jacques Dupont has aptly shown that from chapter 4 on in 2 Corinthians, Paul often uses terms from Greek philosophy. Leaving aside chapter 4, let us concentrate on the present text.

First of all, let us note the verb "to be confident" *(tharrein)*. It was a favorite with the Stoics, Epictetus for instance, but it is also found in Plato in relation to the problem of death. To quote Dupont,[51] "According to the *Phaedo,* the foundation of our confidence in the face of death is the conviction that the soul is immortal and imperishable, 'The real philosopher has reason to be of good cheer when he is about to die' [*tharrein mellōn apothaneisthai*]."[52] Likewise, the idea that one lives on earth, with one's body, as if in exile from one's own homeland, is also found in writers influenced by Platonic thought. For instance, one reads in Philo of Alexandria, "For in reality every soul of a wise man has heaven for its country, and looks upon earth as a strange land, and considers the house of wisdom [its] own home; but the house of the body, a lodging-house, [in] which it proposes to sojourn for a while [*oi kai parepidēmein oietai*]."[53] And also, "God does not grant to the man who loves virtue to dwell in the body as in his own native land, but only to sojourn in it as in a foreign country."[54] Philo also writes, "All the wise men mentioned in the books of Moses are represented as sojourners . . . looking upon the heavenly country in which they have the rights of citizens as their native land, and [upon] the earthly abode in which they dwell for a while as a foreign land."[55] Paul's words in verses 6 and 8 have an unmistakably philosophical tone, and more precisely, a Platonic tone.

We shall therefore not be surprised to see Paul accepting here a distinction between the soul and the body. We live in our body as if in exile, away from the Lord, and we prefer to

---

[51] Dupont, *ΣΥΝ ΧΡΙΣΤΩΙ,* 159. See also Grundmann, article "tharrein" in the TWNT, 3:26.

[52] Plato, *Phaedo* 63; see 88; 95; 114; in Plato, *Dialogues* (all references to the *Dialogues* are taken from this edition).

[53] Philo, *De Agricultura* 14.65, in *Works.*

[54] Philo, *Quis rerum divinarum heres sit* 54.267, in *Works.*

[55] Philo, *De confusione linguarum* 17.76–82, in *Works.*

leave the body in order to go and stay with the Lord. Our body is a temporary dwelling which we leave after death without losing our personality since we are going to live near Christ. True, Paul does not explicitly speak here of our soul, but he postulates a principle of psychic life in us which is not the body and which will be separated from the body. This principle cannot be anything but the soul of which Greek philosophy speaks. Let us observe another thing. For Paul now, there is no question of going down to Sheol as a wan shade, still less of entirely disappearing into the dust of the earth; humans go to join Christ, to dwell with Christ. All this no longer has anything in common with the Semitic concept of death.

The same idea will reappear later on in Paul's letter to the Philippians (1:21-23), where the word "flesh" means "body":

> For to me, living is Christ and dying is gain. If I am to live in the flesh, that means fruitful labor for me; and I do not know which to prefer. I am hard pressed between the two: my desire is to depart and be with Christ, for that is far better; but to remain in the flesh is more necessary for you.

The Problem of the Body

So, Paul has adopted a theme of Platonic philosophy: at the end of earthly life, the soul does not die but goes to join Christ and live with him. But what about the body? Here Paul modifies Platonic spiritualism by means of Semitic realism. The soul finds a body waiting for it in heaven. Paul intimated as much in the first verse of 2 Corinthians 5.

> For we know that if the earthly tent we live in is destroyed, we have a building from God, a house not made with hands, eternal in the heavens.

a) Paul contrasts our earthly house, which is destroyed, with a house waiting for us in heaven. The first term of this pair causes no difficulty in interpretation: it is the body which is meant here. Paul calls it a house as does the Platonic theme he has adopted: we inhabit our body while waiting to leave it behind and go to join Christ in heaven (vv. 6, 8). The term "tent," well known to Greek philosophy[56] (see also Wis 9:15), suggests perhaps precariousness: it is easier to leave a tent than a house. It can also connote the idea that our earthly life is only a journey toward our true heavenly homeland, as in Hebrews 11:9-10:

> By faith [Abraham] stayed for a time in the land he had been promised, as in a foreign land, living in tents, as did Isaac and Jacob, who were heirs with him of the same promise. For he looked forward to the city that has foundations, whose architect and builder is God.

Lastly, let us note that the adjective *epigeios* recalls the fact that the body is formed from the earth (Gen 2:7), as we saw when we studied 1 Corinthians 15. But above all, let us remember that in *Phaedo,* Plato too says that the body is *epigeios,* "earthy," an expression that Wisdom 9:15 picks up when speaking of an "earthy tent" *(geōdēs skēnos).* Everything leads us to believe that by joining the words "earth" and "tent," Paul has this text of Wisdom in mind.

b) But what does Paul mean by this "house" that awaits us in heaven? For André Feuillet,[57] he would mean the body of Christ. To support his position, Feuillet appeals to the word of Jesus as recorded in Mark 14:58, "I will destroy this temple that is made with hands, and in three days I will build another, not made with hands." The two texts indeed have in common the verb "to destroy" (but not under the same form), the words from the same root "building" and "to build," and finally the adjective "made with hands." But this term is used neither in Matthew 26:61 nor in John 2:19—and it is more than probable that it was not part of Jesus' actual words—but only in Mark, maybe due to Paul's influence,[58] although it is likely that Paul did not know of it. Thus, the comparison between the texts of Paul and Mark becomes less significant. And what should we think of this idea that the risen body of

---

[56] See Dupont, *ΣΥΝ ΧΡΙΣΤΩΙ,* 141–145.
[57] Feuillet, "La demeure."
[58] See Boismard, *Mark,* 203.

Christ would become the "house" where all the Christians' souls go to dwell after their death? For J.A.T. Robinson, this word would mean the Church, body of Christ, that the believers would join. But why search so far afield? The examination of the expressions used here shows that Paul means to say that a new body awaits us in heaven, a house in which we shall live as soon as we leave our earthly body.

Indeed, let us note that the terms of the two parts of the sentence form an antithetic parallelism: our "earthly tent" and a "heavenly dwelling," "destroyed" and "eternal," "tent" and "building." This antithetic parallelism must pertain to two realities of the same kind: our earthly body and our body awaiting us in heaven. Let us pay special attention to the opposition between "earthly" and "in the heavens." It recalls that expressed by Paul in 1 Corinthians 15 about the resurrection. In verse 42, one sows an "earthly" body and a "heavenly" body rises (we have explained this: what rise are beings whose nature is heavenly from now on). In verse 49, "Just as we have borne the image of the man of dust, we will also bear the image of the man of heaven." Therefore, at the resurrection, we shall pass from an "earthly" nature to a "heavenly" nature. This will be the destiny even of all those still alive at the time of Christ's return; they will be transformed into "heavenly" beings. But for the Paul of 1 Corinthians 15, the beings to be transformed are beings of flesh and blood; therefore, he believes that our physical being, our body as we would say now, will be transformed into a heavenly being. It becomes clear that in 2 Corinthians 5:1, it is a "heavenly" body that awaits us in heaven.

c) Is such an idea conceivable on Paul's part?[59] Before becoming a Christian, Paul was a convinced Pharisee, Gamaliel's student (Acts 22:2; 23:6). Now, the Jewish historian Flavius Josephus gives us this piece of information, "[The Pharisees] say that all souls are incorruptible, but the souls of good men are only removed into other bodies,–but that the souls of bad

---

[59] Karl Barth thought so, according to Cullmann, *Immortalité*, 66 (he quotes *Dogmatik*, II, 1, pp. 698ff.; III, 2, pp. 524ff. and 714ff.).

men are subject to eternal punishment" (*War* 1.8.14).[60] The Pharisees, or at least some among them,[61] believed in metempsychosis, just like Plato and Pythagoras. All that Paul would have done was transpose the Pharisees' belief. For them, the soul of the just was to find a new body on earth; for Paul, a new body in heaven. For him as for the Pharisees, the soul would pass from one body into another.

It is also interesting to note that this idea of the soul finding another body in heaven after leaving the earthly body behind is also mentioned in the Christian sections of the Jewish apocryphal book the *Ascension of Isaiah*. One of the first Christian interpolations appears in 3:13–4:22, perhaps dating back to the end of the first century. As for chapters 6–11, entirely Christian, they would have been composed later on, in the course of the second century.[62] In 4:16, on the topic of the second coming of Christ, one reads:

> But the saints will accompany the Lord with their robes that are stored in the seventh heaven. Those whose spirits are clothed will accompany the Lord; they will go down and be present in the world, and the Lord will strengthen those who will be found in their bodies, assembled with the saints in the robes of saints. . . . and, after that, they will go up in their robes and their bodies will be left behind in the world.

What do these robes signify? Michael A. Knibb[63] comments on 1:5, where they are already mentioned, "These heavenly robes which the saints put on after their death are a symbol of their transformed state," and to illustrate this point, he refers, among other texts, to 2 Corinthians 5:1-4. Other passages of this apocryphal book specify what the author means by these "robes"; thus in 9:9, "And there, [in the seventh heaven] I saw Enoch and all those stripped of their robes of

[60] Translation A. Pelletier, adopted by Puech, *La Croyance*, 213.

[61] Indeed, in another text (*Ant.* 18.1.3), Josephus attributes to the Pharisees belief in both the immortality of the soul and the resurrection. See Acts 23:6.

[62] For this information, see Knibb, "Martyrdom," 147–150.

[63] Ibid., 157.

flesh, and I saw them clothed with their robes from on high and they were like the angels who stand there in great glory." A little before this passage, Isaiah had heard the heavenly voice tell him, "When, by the will of God, you come up here out of your body, you will receive the robe you have seen, and you will also see other robes kept here, and then you will be the equal of angels who are in the seventh heaven" (8:14-15). All the robes with which the saints will be clothed immediately after their death are already prepared in the seventh heaven.

What is the nature of this body where the soul comes to dwell as in an incorruptible house? We have no reason to think that on this point, Paul had changed his mind since 1 Corinthians 15. He thinks of a body no longer "earthy" but "glorious," that is, a body whose nature is heavenly, more or less identical with the stars of heaven.

The Fear of Death

Verses 2-4 are difficult.

> 2. And in this earthly state we do indeed groan,
> 3. longing to put on our heavenly home over the present one; if indeed we are to be found clothed rather than stripped bare.
> 4. Yes, indeed, in this present tent, we groan under the burden, not that we want to be stripped of covering, but because we want to be covered with a second garment on top, so that what is mortal in us may be swallowed up by life (NJB).

Commentators have interpreted these verses in different ways. Here is the interpretation that seems best to us. To understand this text, we must first go back to what Paul wrote in 1 Corinthians (15:51-53):

> Listen, I will tell you a mystery! We will not all die, but we will all be changed, in a moment, in the twinkling of an eye. . . . the dead will be raised imperishable, and we will be changed. For this perishable body must put on imperishability, and this mortal body must put on immortality. . . . Then the saying that is written will be fulfilled: "Death has been swallowed up in victory."

There is evident kinship between this text and 2 Corinthians 5:2-4. Nevertheless, it is noteworthy that Paul no longer speaks of resurrection since, as we have seen, he has adopted the Greek theme of immortality. But the question concerning those still alive at the time of the eschatological event remains the same. Paul still hopes to be alive when Christ comes back to effect the great transformation which will usher in the new world: all that is corruptible and mortal will put on incorruptibility and immortality so that death will be definitively overcome. This hope is expressed in verse 3, ". . . if indeed, we are to be found clothed rather than stripped bare." Indeed, the adjective "naked" *(gumnos)* was a technical term of Platonic philosophy designating the soul separated from its body. For example, one reads in Plato's *Cratylus* (403) that humans fear the soul might go to Pluto "denuded of the body" *(gumnē tou sōmatos)*. And Philo of Alexandria in *Legum Allegoriarum* (2.59) juxtaposes the two adjectives, "naked" and "bodiless" *(gumnē kai asōmatos)*. In verse 3, Paul means to say: if indeed we are found, at the time of the eschatological event, still clothed with our body and not having left it as those who are dead have done (5:6, 8).

In view of all this, let us note the following fact: in verse 1, Paul speaks of our body, whether earthly or heavenly, as of a house *(oikodomē)*; in verse 2, he keeps this image but blends it in a rather strange fashion with that of a garment one "puts on," as if one could "put on" a building, a house. This incoherence comes from the fact that from verse 2 on, he repeats the theme he had treated in 1 Corinthians 15:51-53: we "put on" incorruptibility, immortality. But when taking up the theme of 1 Corinthians 15, Paul slightly modifies its vocabulary. In 1 Corinthians, he simply spoke of "putting on" *(endusasthai)* incorruptibility. Here, he uses the same verb but with the prefix *epi (ependusasthai)*, which means "upon"; we must therefore translate "to clothe on top." The meaning of the passage then becomes clear. Paul hopes that the eschatological event will occur in his lifetime[64] because

---

[64] But he seems less sure of it than when he wrote 1 Corinthians.

he will not have had to die, to take off his body, to go un-
clothed. In other words, Paul is afraid of death! Although
this death should allow him to go and live with Christ (vv. 6,
8), it still entails a tearing apart of the being when the soul is
separated from the body. And Paul would want to avoid this
pulling apart. If he is still alive at that time, then he will put
on his immortal body on top of his mortal one. Without his
having had to let go of his mortal body, it will be instantaneously changed into an immortal body. How close to us
does Paul appear here!

Summary

Before leaving the analysis of 2 Corinthians 3 and 5, we
are able to propose the following conclusions. As in 1 Corinthians 15:35-54, Paul distinguishes two different cases, that
of those still alive at the time of the eschatological event and
that of those who died previously. As for those still alive, he
adopts the same position: all will be transformed; their corruptible and mortal bodies will instantaneously put on incorruptibility and immortality. But concerning those already
dead, Paul's position radically changes. In 1 Corinthians
15:35-54, he still held to Semitic anthropology based on
Genesis 2:7 (v. 45; cf. Wis 15:8, 11, 16), which professed the
psychosomatic unity of the human being. At death, humans
go down to Sheol as evanescent shades almost completely
deprived of life, unless they simply return to the dust from
which they came (Gen 3:19). It is only at the return of Christ
that they will rise glorious and incorruptible through the action of Christ playing the part of the life-giving *pneuma* of
which Genesis 2:7 speaks. But by the time he writes 2 Corinthians, Paul has understood that in baptism, we have "put
on" Christ, the life-giving *pneuma,* even in this earthly life.
And having within us this principle of eschatological life
which transforms us "from one degree of glory to another"
(2 Cor 3:17-18; cf. 3:6), we are already risen, which implies
the presence within us of an element capable of already
putting on immortality in this life. As Plato taught, the human
being is made up of a soul and a body. At the end of our

earthly life, only the body disintegrates in the earth. As for the soul, it does not die because it possesses the "guarantee" of the *pneuma* (5:5), but it leaves this corruptible body (5:6-8) in order to go and join Christ. However, in contrast to Plato, Paul believes that it then finds an incorruptible body, heavenly in nature, which awaits it in heaven.

Let us conclude this analysis of 2 Corinthians by quoting from one preface of the Mass of the dead, a gloss on 2 Corinthians 5:1: *Vita mutatur non tollitur. . . . Dissoluta terrestris huius incolatus domo, aeterna in coelis habitatio comparatur* ("Life is not taken away, it is changed. . . . When the body of our earthly dwelling lies in death, we gain an everlasting dwelling place in heaven").

$$\text{———} \quad 5 \quad \text{———}$$

The Fourth Book of Maccabees

Now we must see how Jesus conceived of our victory over death. First, however, we must briefly look at a work which is not part of the canon of the Old Testament but which will be useful in helping us interpret certain sayings of Jesus.

The Fourth Book of Maccabees[65] is a homily of Jewish origin, probably delivered in Antioch on the occasion of the feast that commemorated the martyrdom of the seven brothers and their mother. The dates proposed vary from the time of the emperor Claudius (about 40–54) to that of Hadrian (about 125). It is attributed to Flavius Josephus.

This fourth book presents obvious analogies with 2 Maccabees, which we studied above (see pp. 18–22). However, although it repeats some of the latter's themes on the martyrdom of the seven brothers and their mother, it never speaks of resurrection. And yet, it knows that a life awaits the martyrs after their death because it upholds a Platonic anthropology, with a distinction between the soul and the body.

Immortality Promised to the Martyrs

For the author of 4 Maccabees, the person faithful to God obtains eternal life with God at the very moment of

---

[65] See Dupont-Sommer, *Le Quatrième;* Hadas, *Third Macc.*

death. The seven brothers affirm this several times. The most interesting text is 18:23:

> But the sons of Abraham with their victorious mother are gathered together into the chorus of the fathers, and have received pure and immortal souls from God [*psuchas hagias kai athanatous*].

For the martyrs, there is no question of being raised after having gone down to Sheol, but of possessing an immortal soul which rejoins the chorus of the fathers awaiting them near God. Who are these fathers? Obviously, the patriarchs of the Old Covenant who are supposed to be already with God: "They knew also that those who die for the sake of God live to God [*zōsin tōi theōi*], as do Abraham and Isaac and Jacob and all the patriarchs" (16:25) and "Abraham and Isaac and Jacob will welcome us, and all the fathers will praise us" (13:17).

For the author of the homily, the seven brothers are already with God without having had to wait for any eschatological event, as it is stated in 17:17:

> The tyrant himself and all his council marveled at their endurance, because of which they now [*nun*] stand before the divine throne and live the life of eternal blessedness [*makarion aiōna*].

Whereas the author of 2 Maccabees spoke of resurrection, the author of 4 Maccabees speaks of immortality. What the tyrant can destroy is the body, but the soul is immortal. About the seven brothers, the writer can say in 14:5-10:

> But all of them, as if running the course toward immortality [*athanasias*], hastened to death by torture. Just as the hands and feet are moved in harmony with the guidance of the mind, so those holy youths, as though moved by an immortal [*athanatou*] spirit of devotion, agreed to go to death for its sake. . . . For the power of fire is intense and swift, and it consumed their bodies [*dieluen ta sōmata*] quickly.

And of the mother, it is said in 16:13 (cf. 7:3):

On the contrary, as though having a mind like adamant and giving rebirth for immortality [*eis athanasian anatiktousa*] to the whole number of her sons, she implored them and urged them on to death for the sake of religion.

Since the soul is immortal, there is no longer death in the strict sense of the word. As soon as the body dies, the soul goes to join the patriarchs near God and death is no longer anything but an appearance. One of the brothers says, "Let us not fear him who thinks he is killing us [*ton dokounta apokteinein*]" (13:14), and the author of the book writes that they believed "that they, like our patriarchs Abraham, Isaac and Jacob, do not die to God, but live to God [*zōsin tōi theōi*]" (7:19).

Stoicism and Platonism

The Fourth Book of Maccabees without doubt contains a panegyric of the seven martyred brothers and their mother, but it is also a "thoroughly philosophical" treatise *(philoso-phōtaton logon)*—as the author warns us in 1:1—in which he takes the opportunity to exalt the power of reason over the passions of the soul and the body and over all feelings, even the noblest, like the love of a mother for her children. The Stoic influence is very strong.[66] But for everything concerning the life of the soul after the death of the body, the Platonic stamp is undeniable. As André Dupont-Sommer writes, ". . . [the author's] doctrine of the soul and immortality bears the deep imprint of Plato's ideas" (*Le Quatrième*, 44). And, similarly, Moses Hadas, "There is not the slightest doubt that our author is a Platonist" (*Third Macc*, 117).

---

[66] See Hadas, *Third Macc*, 115–118.

6

The Teaching of Christ

We must now ask ourselves how Jesus understood our victory over death: under the form of "resurrection," under the form of "immortality," or under a form that would represent a blend of the two? Was he faithful to a Semitic anthropology that conceived of the human being in its psychosomatic unity? In this case, he would have thought that, at death, humans would go down to Sheol as shades deprived of life who awaited the day on which God would raise them by giving them back the physical elements necessary for the good functioning of their intellectual faculties. Or else, following the Pharisees, had he adopted the Greek notion of the human being as composed of soul and body? In this case, he would have thought that, at death, only the body would disintegrate in the earth while the soul, immortal,[67] would live on and alone would receive its eschatological destiny. But would he not have thought, as it is routinely taught today, that the immortal soul would receive in a certain sense its eschatological destiny, but at the same time would be waiting for the last day when it would be given back its body, which is necessary to its substantial integrity? In order to answer these questions, we shall analyze first the texts of the Synoptic tradition and

[67] In virtue of a gift from God.

100

then those of the Johannine tradition, which present a particular problem.

THE SYNOPTIC TRADITION

If one asked people in what conceptual framework Jesus envisaged our victory over death, the greatest number, including seasoned exegetes,[68] would answer without hesitation "in that of resurrection"; and they would refer us to the narrative in Mark 12:18-27 and to parallels in which Jesus is shown defending belief in a future resurrection in discussions with the Sadducees. But things are not so simple and by probing into Jesus' words, we shall reach quite different conclusions.

In principle, in this kind of study, it would be necessary to examine each text to ascertain whether it is reasonably possible to attribute to Jesus the "saying" in question. But such a study would lead us too far from our subject. However, we shall see that in the Gospels, there are so many texts going back to different traditions while converging toward the same meaning that we can have the quasi-certainty of attaining the teaching of Jesus in its essentials.

The Body and the Soul

In the first place, here is a text of the twofold tradition[69] which shows that Jesus seemed to have accepted the Platonic distinction between the soul and the body:

Matt 10:28	*Luke 12:4-5*
	I tell you, my friends,
Do not fear	do not fear

---

[68] See, among others, Puech, *La Croyance*, 243ff.

[69] We shall follow the classic division: "threefold tradition" when the texts are in Matthew, Mark, and Luke; "twofold tradition" when the texts are present only in Matthew and Luke; "particular traditions" when the texts appear either in Matthew or Luke.

those who kill the body	those who kill the body, and after that
but cannot kill the soul;	can do nothing more. But I will warn you whom to fear;
rather fear him who can destroy both soul and body in hell.	fear him who, after he has killed, has authority to cast into hell.

Matthew's text is the clearer because it explicitly distinguishes the soul from the body. Even though the body is killed, the soul is not and therefore continues to live, and certainly to live without the body since the latter has been put to death and therefore has been destroyed. Luke's text is less precise. The additions "I tell you, my friends," and "but I will warn you whom to fear" are surely Luke's glosses because they bear the stamp of the Lukan style. But the fundamental idea is the same even though Luke does not speak explicitly of the soul. The phrase "and after that can do nothing more" supposes that once they have killed the body, the persecutors cannot put to death another part of the human being, which can only be the soul. What did the source common to Matthew and Luke say exactly? Is it Matthew who completed the original text by explicitly mentioning the soul? Is it Luke who simplified the original logion? It is difficult to say. In any case, this logion presupposed, at least implicitly, a real distinction between the soul and body, only the latter being killed by the persecutors.

What becomes of the soul after death? Jesus does not say here, but he will tell us in other circumstances.

To Lose One's Life in Order to Keep It

Another word of Jesus will allow us to confirm the conclusions deduced from the preceding logion. It too suggests a context of persecution. It has the advantage of having been transmitted—with variations we shall analyze later on—in the threefold tradition (Mark 8:35; Matt 16:25; Luke 9:24), in the twofold tradition (Matt 10:39; Luke 17:33), as well as in the Johannine tradition (John 12:25). We could not ask for more.

Here is the text we read in Mark 8:35 and Luke 9:24; the text is identical in both evangelists if we except two Lukan variants without significance for us:

> For those who want to save their life will lose it,
> and those who lose their life for my sake, and for the sake of the gospel, will save it.

The general idea of the second part of the logion is clear: those who will have accepted death because they acknowledged Jesus as the Christ will save their life, that is, remain alive. This paradoxical statement obviously presupposes in humans the presence of two distinct elements, one which can be put to death by the persecutor, the other which goes on living. Such a duality is absent from Semitic anthropology; it is part of Greek anthropology: the persecutor kills the body but the soul does not die.

Now, let us look at the texts in more detail. The four evangelists agree on the verb's having a negative meaning, that of "losing" one's life. But in Greek, the verb *apollumi* can take on two nuances, "to destroy" or "to lose." In 16:25 as well as in 10:39, Matthew has kept the nuance of "losing," hence its counterpart "finding": those who lose their life will find it. However, he differs from the other three evangelists, and we will not take his text into account.

Let us now compare the text of Mark 8:35 (Luke 9:24 is parallel to it) with that of Luke 17:33:

Mark 8:35	*Luke 17:33*
For those who want to save their life will lose it, and those who lose their life for my sake will save it.	Those who try to make their life secure will lose it, but those who lose their life will keep it.

In the first part of the logion, we have the verb "to want" in Mark and the verb "to try" in Luke. These two verbs can translate the same Aramaic word *(baʿaʾ)*, which has both meanings. In the second part of the logion, Mark has "to save" *(sōzein)* while Luke has "to keep" *(zōogonein)*. Contrary to the Hebrew, the Aramaic does not have a specific verb for "to save"; it uses one of the forms (intensive or factitive) of the verb "to live," which therefore means "to keep alive."[70] This is exactly the meaning of the verb Luke uses, "to keep alive."[71] This meaning is confirmed by the text from John 12:25, "Those who hate their life in this world will keep [*phulassei*] it for eternal life." Here, we have again Mark and Luke giving two different, and exact, translations of the same Aramaic verb. In addition, the Syriac versions—Syriac being a language closely akin to Aramaic—of Mark 8:35 and Luke 17:33 have practically the same translation.

It seems that Luke 17:33 has better preserved the original context of the logion. This context deals with the catastrophe which will mark the end of the world, similar to the fire which fell on Sodom as recorded in Genesis 19. In verse 32, Luke explicitly mentions Lot's wife. In Genesis 19:17, Lot is warned, "save your life" *(sōze tēn psuchēn;* LXX), that is, if you want to remain alive, flee to the mountains.

In view of all this, here is the conclusion we can draw from this word of Jesus. First of all, it is attested, with some variants, in the threefold tradition, the twofold tradition, and the Johannine tradition, a fact which is a guarantee of authenticity. Another favorable point is that in the Gospels it reveals its source in Aramaic, the language Jesus spoke.

Because of its paradoxical formulation, this saying can be understood only within the framework of Greek anthropology, which distinguished two components in human nature, the soul and the body, in contrast to Semitic anthropology. Those who accept death for the sake of Christ keep their life; they die in their body, but their soul remains alive. A point

[70] And also "to give life back."

[71] This is the meaning Bauer–Aland gives, *Vörterbuch*, col. 690: *am Leben erhalten*. See Acts 7:19, in the passive voice, and also, LXX Exod 1:17, 18, 22; LXX Judg 8:19; in these texts, the verb *zōogonein* translates one of the forms of the Hebrew verb meaning "to live."

added by John is that they keep their life "for eternal life," as we will learn from other sayings of Jesus to be analyzed later on. On the other hand, those who want to save themselves by denying Christ will lose their life, in the sense that God will deliver them to hell, soul and body (see Matt 10:28, pp. 101–102). As for the just, the logion defines their destiny in terms of immortality, not in terms of resurrection (as Daniel saw it).

To Enter Into Life

Let us now look at the three-part saying of Jesus on the subject of scandal in Mark 9:42-48 and Matthew 18:6-8. We limit ourselves to quoting the first part of this saying in Mark:

> If your hand causes you to stumble, cut it off; it is better for you to enter life maimed than to have two hands and to go to hell, to the unquenchable fire.

According to antithetic parallelism, the entrance into life is an eschatological event, as is the condemnation to hell. What must we understand by this "life" into which the righteous are to enter? Marie-Joseph Lagrange[72] very aptly comments: "*Ē zōē* is the real life, the afterlife; this term was known to the Psalms of Solomon. . . . It was life in God, as Wisdom says . . . the life of the world to come according to transcendent Rabbinism." But when will this entrance into life occur? Let us again quote Lagrange, who continues, "The moment when one enters into one or the other of the two regions is not specified, but it can only be the moment that follows death."

In the third part of Jesus' saying according to Mark, instead of "enter life," one reads "enter the kingdom." The two expressions are equivalent; we shall possess the true life in the eschatological realm (see Mark 10:17, 23-25).

This saying must be understood within a perspective of immortality, not of resurrection, since one enters life, or the

[72] Lagrange, *Marc*, 251.

realm, as soon as one has died. The body dies but the soul enters eternal life. We must not focus too closely on the expression "to enter life maimed"; obviously, Jesus does not mean to say that we shall lack one hand or one foot or one eye when we live in God's realm; he wants simply to say that we shall be maimed only at the time we enter the realm. Later on, we shall come back to the problem of the "body" of the just in the world to come.

Lukan Traditions

Now let us study two texts peculiar to Luke, which must derive from traditions only he made use of.

– The first text is the word which Jesus, nailed to the cross, addresses to the good thief (23:42-43). The latter asks, "Jesus, remember me when you come into your kingdom." And the answer comes, "Today you will be with me in Paradise." It is possible to discourse at length on what the "paradise" Jesus speaks of is. It does not matter. The essential is to observe that Jesus does not promise a resurrection to the good thief but takes for granted that his soul, which will escape death on the cross, will continue to live and will find itself in paradise. "Today" shows that there is no interval between the death on the cross and the entrance into paradise. For Luke, if the good thief can continue to live even after the death of his body, it is because of his soul, the only part of him capable of enjoying immortality.

– In the parable of Lazarus and the rich man (16:19-31), we see that as soon as he dies, Lazarus is carried by the angels into Abraham's bosom. He too continues to live after the death of his body. If the resurrection is mentioned in verse 31, it is in a completely hypothetical manner and refers to sinners who presumably would be in Hades. Besides, we see here that Hades is reserved solely for sinners; there is no question of the righteous going down to it.

The Patriarchs

One reads in Luke 13:26-29, a text of the twofold tradition (see Matt 8:11-12) whose context is better preserved by Luke:

26. Then you will begin to say, "We ate and drank with you, and you taught in our streets."
27. But he will say, "I do not know where you come from; go away from me, all you evildoers!"
28. There will be weeping and gnashing of teeth when you see Abraham and Isaac and Jacob and all the prophets in the kingdom of God, and you yourselves thrown out.
29. Then people will come from east and west, from north and south, and will eat in the kingdom of God.

The mention of patriarchs and prophets recalls the developments we have seen in 4 Maccabees: the patriarchs, who already live with God, welcome the martyrs. Here, the author speaks of those Jews who are contemporaries of Jesus but who refuse to believe in him. They rely on their past acquaintance with Jesus to gain them entrance into the reign; instead, they will be thrown out of it, but not without having had time to see the patriarchs already installed near God. The viewpoint seems to be the same as in 4 Maccabees: as soon as they died, the patriarchs and all the prophets entered the kingdom and enjoy God's presence. We shall see this theme again a little later.

The Return of Christ

All the texts analyzed up to now show that Jesus conceived of our victory over death in terms of immortality. But would he not have thought also of a resurrection of the body, to take place when he came back to earth? At this point, let us reread what has come to be called Jesus' "eschatological discourse."

– An early form of this discourse has been transmitted to us in the threefold tradition. The return of Christ is described in Mark 13:24-27, Matthew 24:29-31, and Luke 21:25-28. In Mark's text, after having spoken of the cosmic[73] signs which will precede this return, Jesus adds:

[73] These must not be taken literally. On Pentecost, Peter quotes Joel 3:1-5, a text that speaks of similar cosmic signs, and he introduces the quotation with these words, "This is what was spoken by

> 26. Then they will see "the Son of Man coming in clouds" with great power and glory.
> 27. Then he will send out the angels, and gather his elect from the four winds, from the ends of the earth to the ends of heaven.

If Jesus had thought of a resurrection of the dead, or at least of a resurrection of their bodies at the end of time, it was here that he was bound to mention it, especially since he announces his return by quoting Daniel 7:13 and since, in verse 19, he had made a precise allusion to Daniel 12:1.[74] Should he not have said, as Paul did in 1 Thessalonians 4:16 and 1 Corinthians 15:52, that his return will effect *first* the resurrection of the dead? Instead, he speaks only of the gathering of the elect by quoting Zechariah 2:6 and Deuteronomy 30:4. Now, these two Old Testament texts concern just the Hebrews who will have been scattered to the four corners of the world and whom God will bring back to the Promised Land so that they may share in the eschatological reign. Christ does not envision a resurrection of the dead, still less a resurrection of the body at the time of his eschatological return.

Let us note that Luke does not even allude to this gathering of the elect.

– Shall we be luckier when we reread the other form of the eschatological discourse, which is given us in the twofold tradition, in Luke 17:22-37 (see Matt 24:26-27, 37-41)? Jesus mentions his return in verses 24, 26, and 30, but he especially insists on the catastrophe that will befall the world on that day, a catastrophe similar to the Flood (vv. 26-27) and the destruction of Sodom by fire (vv. 29-30). Jesus considers only the fate of those who will still be living when he returns. Making reference to the narrative in Genesis 19:17, he pro-

---

the prophet Joel." Now, on that day, there were none of these cosmic signs. For Peter, it was simply a way of saying that the whole cosmos took part in divine action, here in the outpouring of the Holy Spirit.

[74] Let us recall that Dan 12:2 is one of the clearest texts concerning the resurrection of the dead.

nounces the words studied above, "Those who try to make their life secure will lose it, but those who lose their life will keep it." When speaking of his eschatological return, Jesus speaks in a way that presupposes belief in immortality but does not say one word about a resurrection of the dead.

This should not surprise us because in all the sayings we have analyzed, he sees our victory over death in terms of immortality, not of resurrection.

The Discussion with the Sadducees

However, has not Jesus defended the notion of a resurrection of the dead against the Sadducees who denied it (Mark 12:18-27; Matt 22:23-33; Luke 20:27-40). This is the question which we must now address.

To negate the belief in a resurrection of the dead, the Sadducees bring to Jesus the following argument. According to the law of the levirate (Deut 25:5-6), when a married man dies without having had children, his brother must marry the widow so as to raise a posterity for the deceased. They imagine the case of seven brothers who, having married the same woman, die in succession. Then, they ask, whose wife will she be at the resurrection? Here is Jesus' answer according to Mark:

> 24. Jesus said to them, "Is not this the reason you are wrong, that you know neither the scriptures nor the power of God?
> 25. For when they rise from the dead, they neither marry nor are given in marriage, but are like angels in heaven.
> 26. And as for the dead being raised, have you not read in the book of Moses in the story about the bush, how God said to him, 'I am the God of Abraham, the God of Isaac, and the God of Jacob'?
> 27. He is God not of the dead, but of the living; you are quite wrong."

However, does this text in its present form give us the earliest expression of the Synoptic tradition? Is it possible that an older text was modified by the addition of the theme of the resurrection? Here is what we wrote in our commentary on the

Synoptic Gospels (to know whether this narrative was to be placed or not in the perspective of Jesus' teaching on the topic of our victory over death was not our concern at that time):[75]

> In the three Synoptics, Jesus' response is a composite. The argument from Exodus 3:6 (Mark 12:26 and parallels) obviously corresponds to Jesus' interrogation in Mark 12:24 and the parallel texts ". . . know neither the scriptures? . . ." The detail concerning the fact that people who are raised do not marry (Mark 12:25 and parallels) appears to be an addition; besides, verse 26a of Mark (and parallels), "and as for the dead being raised," is a redactor's means of returning to the narrative, interrupted by the gloss of verse 25.

We added, "At a later period, some people thought that Jesus had not answered exactly the objection of the Sadducees, and they inserted Mark 12:25 and parallels in order to fill in what was regarded as incomplete."

Here is the original text insofar as we were able to reconstruct it:

> 24. Jesus said to them, "Is not this the reason you are wrong, that you do not know the scriptures?
> 26b. Have you not read . . . how God said, 'I am the God of Abraham, the God of Isaac, and the God of Jacob?'
> 27. He is God not of the dead, but of the living; you are quite wrong."

It is easy to see that by omitting from the account as it now stands everything which concerns the resurrection of the dead, one obtains an answer given by Jesus which is completely coherent, if rather elliptical. Furthermore, this answer is in conformity with the theme of immortality as it appears in Jesus' words analyzed above. For Jesus begins by quoting the text of Exodus 3:6, "I am the God of Abraham, the God of Isaac, and the God of Jacob." P. Dreyfus[76] has proved by means of abundant documentation drawn either from the Old Testament or from Jewish literature that the expression "God of . . ." does not mean primarily "the one adored by so

---

[75] Boismard, *Synopse 2,* 348.
[76] Dreyfus, "L'argument."

and so," but has a salvific connotation and means "the one who has protected so and so." One could see the two locutions "God of . . ." and "Savior of . . ." as equivalent. As a consequence, God cannot be a God of the dead, but only a God of the living (v. 27). How could God claim to be, without a cruel irony, the savior of dead people? If they are dead, God has not saved them; on the contrary, God has abandoned them at the very time they had the greatest need of God's protection, that is, at the time of their death.

Dreyfus concludes: "If Abraham is dead *forever,* the help that God had guaranteed him by claiming the title 'God of Abraham' has been a mockery. Therefore, Abraham *must live again."* We would have here a proof of the resurrection of the dead. For his part, Lagrange[77] writes:

> God does not abandon God's own to death: Abraham, Isaac, and Jacob were therefore still alive. Now—and this answers the second difficulty—the Hebrews did not imagine death as a liberation of the soul allowing it to go back to the Ideas, in Platonic fashion. The dead were in Sheol, where they led a very imperfect life; if God is really the God of the living, God will one day free from the dwelling of the dead those who had been and remained God's friends, in order to renew with them a more intimate relationship.

Lagrange thinks that "the Hebrews did not imagine death as a liberation of the soul," and this is why he rejects the idea that the patriarchs were already with God, and not in Sheol. But like the Pharisees, Jesus believed in the immortal afterlife of souls freed from their bodies; we have abundantly proved this by studying the other sayings in which Jesus asserted that the soul survives after death. For him, therefore, Abraham, Isaac, and Jacob are still alive, not in Sheol as shades deprived of genuine life, but as souls enjoying bliss with God. We have seen that this is the idea expressed by the author of 4 Maccabees: the patriarchs Abraham, Isaac, and Jacob receive the martyrs' souls, in God.

Luke seems to have perceived the closeness of his thought to 4 Maccabees. In 20:38, he completes Jesus' saying in this

---

[77] Lagrange, *Marc,* 320.

way, "Now he is God not of the dead, but of the living, for
to him all of them are alive [*pantes gar autōi zōsin*]." At this
point, it is good to go back to the text of 4 Maccabees 7:19,
"since they believe that they, like our patriarchs Abraham
and Isaac and Jacob, do not die to God, but live to God
[*zōsin tōi theōi*]," as well as 16:25, "They knew also that
those who die for the sake of God live to God [*zōsin tōi
theōi*], as do Abraham and Isaac and Jacob and all the patriarchs." Likewise, in verse 35, Luke adds to the two parallel texts of Mark and Matthew the formula "but those who
are considered worthy [*kataxiōthentes*] of a place in that
age" as in 4 Maccabees 18:3, "[they] were deemed worthy to
share in a divine inheritance."

Finally, let us remind readers that this theme of the patriarchs Abraham, Isaac, and Jacob already being with God
had been expressed by Jesus in Luke 13:26-29 and its parallel in Matthew (see pp. 106–107).

In summary, we encounter the following difficulty:
whereas most of Jesus' sayings recorded in the Gospels show
that he conceived of our victory over death in terms of immortality, not of resurrection, Mark's account in 12:18-27 is
an exception in that it seems that Jesus defends the idea of
resurrection against the Sadducees. But the literary criticism
of the text leads one to think that the specific theme of resurrection was not part of the original narrative. If one ex-
cises it from the saying, one arrives at an answer completely
in accord with the other passages where Jesus speaks of our
victory over death in terms of immortality: Abraham, Isaac,
and Jacob are even now alive with God; therefore, they are
not dead. Thanks to God, the "God of the living," they enjoy
a blessed immortality. The same will be our lot when we de-
part this earthly life.

In Luke 14:14-16, Jesus offers this advice: when you give
a big banquet, invite people who cannot invite you in return;
you will be rewarded "at the resurrection of the righteous."
This could be regarded as another of Jesus' words referring
to the resurrection of the dead. Here, however, Jesus is not
addressing his disciples but an individual, and it is normal
that he should speak in such a way in order to be understood

by his questioner who in all likelihood believed in the resurrection of the righteous.

THE JOHANNINE TRADITION

The Johannine tradition is not homogeneous; certain texts represent our victory over death in terms of immortality, while others clearly affirm that Christ will raise us up at the end of time. Let us examine these texts and see at what conclusion we can arrive.

Realized Eschatology

a) Before looking at some of the Johannine texts, let us recall how Paul's thought evolved. In 1 Corinthians 15:45-54, he tells us that the resurrection of the dead, as well as the transformation of all Christians which imparts immortality, will happen at the return of Christ and under his action: he will act on us as the life-giving breath *(pneuma zōopoioun)* of Genesis 2:7 (LXX). But in 2 Corinthians 3, Paul understands that even in this earthly life, we have received within us Christ, "life-giving breath" (see vv. 6, 17-18), thanks to baptism, and therefore, already in this life, Christ transforms us "from one degree of glory to another"; by putting on Christ, our soul has gained the privilege of becoming immortal: death is henceforth abolished for us. This is what John teaches us as we shall see.

In 20:22, Jesus breathed *(enephusēsen)* on his disciples while saying, "Receive the holy Spirit [*pneuma*]." The verb used here is the same as that found in Genesis 2:7 (LXX), "[God] breathed [*enephusēsen*] on its face a breath of life [*pneuma*] and the human became a living being." Besides, for John (6:63), this breath that comes out of Christ's mouth is "life-giving breath" *(to pneuma zōopoiei)*. Without any doubt, John has in mind the text of Genesis 2:7 when he writes 20:22. It is therefore right after his resurrection that Jesus gives his disciples this "breath" which will endow them with a new life entailing immortality. His disciples receive it even as they are still alive on earth, and not in a hypothetical future. Eschatology is already realized.

If this is so, we can no longer die, in the Semitic sense of the word. Those who listen to Jesus' words and believe in the One who sent him "have eternal life and [do] not come under judgment, but [have] passed [already!] from death to life" (5:24; cf. 1 John 3:14). Those who keep his word "will never see death," "will never taste death" (8:51-52). These are the very expressions, as we have seen, with which Jewish tradition recalled the cases of the patriarch Enoch and prophet Elijah, who had been taken to heaven without going through death. Jesus affirms to Martha, "Everyone who lives and believes in me will never die" (11:26). He is the bread come down from heaven so that those who eat it may never die (6:50). Jesus knows his sheep, he gives them eternal life; they will not perish and no one can snatch them out of his protecting hand (10:28). Hence, since Jesus breathed on his disciples the "life-giving breath" of Genesis 2:7, they can no longer be subjected to death; they are already risen.

This obviously postulates that human nature is made up of a soul and a body. Since it is a fact of experience that the body disappears into the earth, for humans to continue living, for them, in a certain sense, not to die, they must of necessity possess a principle that is not affected by death; and this principle cannot be anything but the soul as Greek philosophy understands it.

b) This question of our victory over death is treated in a deeper manner in the sapiential part of the discourse on the bread of life in 6:35-51a.[78] Jesus first states: "I am the bread of life. Whoever comes to me will never be hungry, and whoever believes in me will never be thirsty." By speaking of the bread which satisfies and (the water) which quenches thirst, Jesus wants to show that he is Wisdom come into the world (see Sir 24:19-21; Prov 9:5; Isa 55:1-3). Now, it is by accepting the teaching of this divine Wisdom that humans will escape death.

[78] We are reusing here the developments in Boismard–Lamouille, *Synopse 3*, 198.

This theme is developed by John in reference to the narratives of Genesis 2–3 on original sin. In the earthly paradise, God had planted two trees, the tree of life and the tree of the knowledge of good and evil (Gen 2:9). For having tasted of this latter tree in spite of God's formal prohibition (2:17; 3:1-7), Adam and Eve were expelled from paradise so that they might not have any further access to the tree of life (3:22-24); they were therefore doomed to die (3:19). However, ancient Jewish traditions stated that this curse weighing down humanity was not without remedy and that God had given to humans a means to find again, if not the tree of life, at least its equivalent. For example, the Targum Neofiti 1 says on Genesis 3:24:

> For the Law is a tree of life for everyone who toils in it and keeps the commandments: he lives and endures like the tree of life in the world to come. The Law is good for all who labor in it in this world like the fruit of the tree of life.[79]

Thus, the observance of the Law gives life to humans in the world to come just as the tree of life did in the earthly paradise. The same theme is found also in the biblical wisdom tradition, but the Law is replaced by Wisdom which, on the one hand, endows humanity with the knowledge lost by Adam and Eve (Wis 10:8-9) and, on the other, has the same salvific power as the tree of life: "[Wisdom] is a tree of life to those who lay hold of her; / those who hold her fast are called happy"[80] (Prov 3:18; cf. 11:30; 13:12; 15:4). To humanity, Wisdom brings as it were an antidote to Adam's sin; it saves humanity from death (Wis 10).

Now let us come back to John's text. In the beginning of the sapiential discourse, Jesus gives his audience to understand that he is "the bread of life," and therefore the Wisdom of God that came into the world (John 6:35). At the end of the same discourse, in 6:51a, he states, "Whoever eats this bread will

---

[79] *Targum Neofiti 1: Genesis*, trans., with apparatus and notes, Martin McNamara, The Aramaic Bible, the Targums, vol. 1A (Collegeville, Minn., 1992).

[80] The text simply says that those who hold onto Wisdom will live for a long time on earth.

live forever [*ean tis phagē . . . zēsetai eis ton aiōna*]." Christ-Wisdom can replace the tree of life; those who eat the bread it gives, who follow its teachings, will live forever. For a long time, commentators have noted that John's expression "the bread of life," which has no equivalent in the rest of the New Testament, could evoke this other expression, "the tree of life" from the Genesis narrative (2:9; 3:22-24). Finally, Jesus declares in 6:37, "And anyone who comes to me I will never drive away." Because they tasted of the tree of the knowledge of good and evil, God threw [*exebalen*] Adam and Eve out of the garden (Gen 3:24; LXX); but now, Christ, the Wisdom of God, the principle of the knowledge of good and evil, will not drive away *(ou mē ekbalō)* those who come to him. He is really the antidote to original sin; he is the living bread that came down from heaven "so that one may eat of it and not die" (6:50).

c) Judaism was waiting for the advent of a new world which would be inaugurated at the resurrection of the just. It distinguished between "this world," in which we live and which is more or less dominated by evil, and "the world to come." It was an eschatology which could be called linear. In John 8:23, Jesus says to the Jews, "You are from below, I am from above; you are of this world, I am not of this world." But now the perception of the two worlds is transposed. To this world is now opposed, not the world to come, but the world above. The world to come is no longer to be placed in an indefinite future; it exists right now "above," that is, in heaven, or in God. Indeed, at death, the soul of each human being leaves its body in order to go near God; the world to come is already established in God.

d) According to Jewish prophetic tradition, the advent of the world to come was to be inaugurated by God's great Judgment in order to separate the righteous from the sinners, the former alone being entitled to have a part in the new world. According to the Jesus of John, the judgment is already accomplished. Christ-Light came into the world and humans were divided into two groups—and in this the judgment consists—some came to the light, others refused to come because their deeds were evil (John 3:18-21).

All these sayings of Jesus can be understood only in the perspective of a victory over death, envisaged as immortality, not as resurrection.

The Future Resurrection

But side by side with these texts, others speak of a future resurrection. In chapter 6, in the discourse on the bread of life, this refrain recurs, "I will raise them up on the last day" (vv. 39, 40, 44, 54). Whereas in 3:18-21 Jesus asserted that the judgment had come, in 12:48b he puts off this judgment to the last day, ". . . on the last day the word that I have spoken will serve as judge." Whereas in 5:24-25 Jesus states that those who listen to his word have "passed from death to life" and therefore are already risen, in 5:28-29 he says, ". . . all who are in their graves will hear his [the Son of Man's] voice and will come out–those who have done good, to the resurrection of life, and those who have done evil, to the resurrection of condemnation" (cf. Dan 12:2).

All these texts can be understood only in the perspective adopted by the prophet Daniel, a perspective of resurrection and not of immortality.

Thus, there exists a tension in John's Gospel between the words of Jesus which envisage our victory over death in terms of immortality and those which envisage it in terms of resurrection. Which are the earlier ones?

Immortality in the Early Gospel of John

As has been recognized by numerous commentators, it is easy to prove that the theme of immortality is primary in John's Gospel and that the theme of resurrection is only secondary. Let us reread the beginning of the dialogue between Jesus and Martha, in 11:21-25a:

> 21. Martha said to Jesus, "Lord, if you had been here, my brother would not have died.
> 22. But even now I know that God will give you whatever you ask of him."

> 23. Jesus said to her, "Your brother will rise again."
> 24. Martha said to him, "I know that he will rise again in the resurrection on the last day."
> 25a. Jesus said to her, "I am the resurrection and the life."

We have here a literary device frequent in the Fourth Gospel: Jesus speaks words that can be understood in two different ways, the proper sense, material, and the figurative sense, spiritual. Mistakenly, the questioner understands the words in the proper or material sense, and Jesus answers by unveiling the true meaning of his words. Similarly, in 3:3-5, Jesus declares to Nicodemus that he must be born again;[81] Nicodemus understands this word in the literal sense and wonders; then Jesus reveals the real meaning of his words: one must be born again of water and Spirit. Likewise, in 4:10-14, Jesus tells the Samaritan woman that he can give her living water; she understands this in the material sense and is astonished; then Jesus tells her that she has to understand this word in the spiritual sense (cf. 4:32-34). The same is true of our passage: Jesus affirms that Lazarus will rise; Martha takes it in the way the Jews did, "I know that he will rise again in the resurrection on the last day"; Jesus rectifies this error by declaring himself to be the resurrection and the life, meaning that whoever believes in him is already risen (5:24) and will never die (8:51). We have here the negation of a resurrection "on the last day" as the Jews understood it.

Let us add a further observation. The text of verses 25-26 seems overburdened. A literary scheme, frequent in John's Gospel, is present here: the use of the formula "I am." Let us compare two passages, 11:25-26 and 8:12.

11:25-26	*8:12*
I am the resurrection and the life.	I am the light of the world.
Those who believe in me, even though they die, will live,	Whoever follows me

---

[81] And not "from above," as it is often understood; the Greek verb can have both meanings.

and everyone who lives	
and believes in me	will never walk in darkness
will never die.	but will have the light of
	life.

One can see how the words which we have indented over-burden the text in comparison with that of 8:12. Besides, they are framed by the redactorial repetition "believe in me." The person who added these words was unaware that Jesus was speaking from the point of view of immortality: he is the resurrection and the life; those who believe in him will never die, they have "passed from death to life" (5:24), they "will never taste death" (8:51). But does not this saying of Jesus contradict our experience, that we must all die one day? Hence the addition, "even though they die, they will live." The hand that added this "correction" to Jesus' word is the same that in the discourse on the bread of life, inserted the refrain "and I will raise them up on the last day."

Here is how we must understand John's text. Jesus affirms to Martha that her brother will rise. Thinking that he refers to the Jewish belief inherited from Daniel, she answers, "I know that he will rise again in the resurrection on the last day." At this point, Jesus rectifies her thought: he himself is the resurrection and the life; those who believe in him will never die. Therefore, it is the theme of immortality that underlies this dialogue, as elsewhere in the Gospels.

CONCLUSION

Whether they are recorded in the Synoptics, according to different traditions which guarantee their authenticity, or in John's Gospel, the sayings of Jesus lead us to draw the same conclusion: for him, our victory over death must be thought of in terms of immortality and not of resurrection. This presupposes that like the Pharisees, Jesus endorsed the Greek distinction between the soul and the body. At the end of earthly life, the body decays in the earth while the soul "enters life" or "the kingdom." In this sense, the soul, which is the seat of the human personality, is immortal. But on this point, Jesus differs from Plato because for him this immortality is a free gift from God: it is because God is the "God of the living" that God spares humans from being engulfed by death at the end of their earthly life.

But what about the body? There is no hint that one is found at the end of time. When Jesus announces his return, he does not envisage any resurrection accompanying this event. However, the realism with which he speaks of our entrance into eternal life leads us to think that for him, the soul does not enter there completely disembodied. It seems that Jesus had adopted a way of thinking similar to Paul's in 2 Corinthians 5:1: the soul joins a "heavenly" body at the very moment it leaves this "earthy" body.

Part Three

THE RISEN CHRIST

The Risen Christ

When reading what the Gospels and the Acts of the Apostles tell us about the Risen Christ, one gets the impression that Jesus' aspect after his resurrection did not essentially differ from the one he had during his earthly life: he converses with his disciples, walks with them, eats in their presence, exactly as he would have done in the past. But one should not be misled by what could be nothing more than a helpful literary device used in the Gospels and Acts to convey more effectively the living reality of Christ come back to life. In the following remarks, we shall not doubt the reality of the appearances of the Risen Christ. But what about their realism?

The Reality of the Appearances

It is impossible to doubt the fact that the Risen Christ appeared to his disciples. About 57 C.E., therefore some twenty-five years after the resurrection, Paul wrote to the faithful in Corinth (1 Cor 15:3-8):

> 3. For I handed on to you as of first importance what I in turn had received: that Christ died for our sins in accordance with the scriptures,
> 4. and that he was buried, and that he was raised on the third day in accordance with the scriptures,

5. and that he appeared to Cephas, then to the twelve.

6. Then he appeared to more than five hundred brothers and sisters at one time, most of whom are still alive, though some have died.

7. Then he appeared to James, then to all the apostles.

8. Last of all, as to one untimely born, he appeared also to me.

The first thing Paul taught the people in Corinth when he evangelized them was the reality of Christ's resurrection, confirmed by his appearances to his disciples. By doing so, Paul has not innovated; he has transmitted what he himself had received from the living tradition of the early Church. Besides, the reality of these appearances can be verified, Paul adds, since most of those who witnessed them are still alive.

According to Acts, we see the reality of the appearances boldly proclaimed to the Jews from the very beginning of the apostolic tradition. To the Jewish crowds gathered in the Jerusalem Temple and astonished at seeing Peter cure a cripple near one of the gates of the Temple (Acts 3:1-15), Peter declares:

13. The God of Abraham, the God of Isaac, and the God of Jacob, the God of our ancestors has glorified his servant Jesus, whom you handed over and rejected in the presence of Pilate, though he had decided to release him.

14. But you rejected the Holy and Righteous One and asked to have a murderer given to you,

15. and you killed the Author of life, whom God raised from the dead. To this we are witnesses.

Like Jesus (Mark 12:26), Peter begins by recalling the text of Exodus 3:6: it is the Savior of the patriarchs who has snatched Jesus from death. And just as Paul will affirm later on that we will all be transformed by the divine "glory" (1 Cor 15:40-54), Peter says that God has glorified his servant Jesus (cf. Isa 52:13). Furthermore, how could the disciples be witnesses of Christ's resurrection if not because Christ, living, appeared to them? This is what Peter will explain to the centurion Cornelius before baptizing him and those with him (Acts 10:39-41):

39. We are witnesses to all that he did both in Judea and Jerusalem. They put him to death by hanging him on a tree;
40. but God raised him on the third day and allowed him *to appear,*
41. not to all the people but to us who were chosen by God *as witnesses,* and who ate and drank with him after he rose from the dead.

This is what Paul will recall later on in the speech he delivered in Antioch of Pisidia (Acts 13:30-31):

But God raised him from the dead; and for many days *he appeared* to those who came up with him from Galilee to Jerusalem, and they are now his witnesses to the people.

Having been the witnesses of the resurrection, thanks to Christ's appearances, the apostles can base their discussions with the Jews on this well-attested fact to refute the incredulity of their hearers (Acts 2:24; 4:10; 5:30).

We do not cast any doubt on the reality of the appearances of the Risen Christ. But what are we to think about their realism?

The Realism of the Appearances

a) In order to evaluate the realism of the appearances, we must first of all notice that when Christ appears, even his most intimate disciples do not recognize him immediately; he must make a gesture, say something that will make him known. When he appears to the eleven, he must show the wounds in his hands and side (John 20:20; cf. Luke 24:38-39). When he appears to Mary Magdalene, she sees him standing (risen) and "she did not know that it was Jesus";[1] she thought he was the gardener, and Jesus had to call her by name, Mary, for her to recognize him (John 20:14-16). In the episode of the two disciples from Emmaus, Jesus joins them, "but their eyes were kept from recognizing him." It is only after Jesus broke the

[1] This fact is the more striking as Mary Magdalene was certainly a close disciple of Christ.

bread in their presence that "their eyes were opened and they recognized him" (Luke 24:16, 31). Likewise, at the time of the miraculous draught of fish, he stands on the lake shore, but they "did not know that it was Jesus." Only at the sight of the miracle does the disciple whom Jesus loved say to Peter, "It is the Lord" (John 21:4-12). As Mark points out in 16:12, he appears "in another form."

b) Let us try to see more precisely what this other form could be. In speaking of the appearances of the Risen Christ, the early Church almost always used the same verb, and most often in the same form (passive aorist), which became a technical term, *ōphthē,* literally "he was seen," but ordinarily translated as "he appeared." It is this verb which occurs five times in the kerygmatic fragment quoted by Paul in 1 Corinthians 15:3-8. When the disciples of Emmaus go back to Jerusalem, the eleven apostles and their companions tell them, "The Lord is risen indeed, and he has appeared [*ōphthē*] to Simon" (Luke 24:34). When Paul, after the vision that overwhelmed him on the way to Damascus, meets the disciple Ananias, the latter tells him, "Brother Saul, the Lord Jesus, who appeared to you [*ho ōphtheis soi*] on your way here . . ." (Acts 9:17). Christ himself had said to Paul, "I have appeared to you [*ōphthēn soi*] for this purpose, to appoint you to serve and testify to the things in which you have seen me and to those in which I will appear to you [*ophthēsomai soi*]" (Acts 26:16). In his discourse at Antioch of Pisidia, Paul declares that God has raised Jesus from the dead, he who has appeared *(ōphthē)* during several days to those who had come with him from Galilee to Jerusalem (Acts 13:30-31). In other texts, the same verb is used, but in the active form (Matt 28:7, 10; Mark 16:7; John 20:18, 25, 29).

This use of the verb *ōphthē* is intentional. To speak of the appearances of the risen Christ, the early Christians did nothing more than repeat the technical term employed in the Septuagint and the New Testament to describe the appearances of God or the angels. In Genesis 12:7, it is said that God appeared *(ōphthē)* to Abraham to make him a promise; the same verb is used by Luke in Acts 7:2 when he recalls this event. Likewise, in Genesis 18:1-2, God appeared *(ōphthē)* again to Abraham, and in this case, God was accompanied by two angels (see 18:22 and 19:1). In his Gospel (see 1:11; 22:43), Luke always uses this verb *(ōphthē)* to say that an angel appeared either to Zechariah, John the Baptist's father, or Jesus himself. The early Christian tradition wanted to thus signify that the Risen Christ now belonged to the heavenly world. This does not simply mean that Christ is now in heaven but, in a much deeper way, as Paul explains in 1 Corinthians 15:40-49 in connection with the risen Christians, that he is no longer made of earth, he is no longer earthly, he has a heavenly substance.

c) Let us go deeper into our analysis. In John's Gospel, when alluding to his resurrection, Jesus declares that he will be "glorified" (12:23; 13:31-32; 17:1; see also 12:16). Does this simply mean that he will receive a special honor[2] from human beings? The meaning is much more profound, as is shown by the prayer Jesus addresses to his Father in 17:5, "So now, Father, glorify me in your own presence with the glory that I had in your presence before the world existed." After his resurrection, Christ will find again the glory he had before the creation of the world. This is a participation in the very glory of God, which the Old Testament often describes as a blinding light.[3] Therefore, Peter can affirm immediately after the resurrection that "the God of Abraham . . . has *glorified* his servant Jesus" (Acts 3:13). We rejoin here the very teaching of Paul in 1 Corinthians concerning the state of risen Christians: they will obtain a "glory," that is, a luminous radiance similar to that of the stars shining in the heavens. And when Paul journeys toward Damascus, he is thrown down by "a light from heaven" while a voice says, "I am Jesus whom you are persecuting" (Acts 9:4-5). Now, Paul placed this appearance on the same footing as those to other disciples (1 Cor 15:5-8). The Risen Christ has therefore become

---

[2] The Greek verb can have this meaning even in John's Gospel.

[3] For all that concerns this divine "glory" and its luminous radiance, we refer the readers to Mollat, "Gloire," 414–415.

a "glorious" being, a being no longer made of earth, but of light.

d) In view of all this, how should we understand the realism of the appearances? Since the Risen Christ no longer belongs to our world made of earthly matter, he no longer is visible to human eyes. This is obvious even in the most "realistic" accounts of appearances. For instance, in the story of the disciples from Emmaus, Jesus walks along with them. The way in which they recognize him is described as follows, "Then their eyes were opened, and they recognized him; and he vanished [*aphantos egeneto*] from their sight" (Luke 24:31). Luke echoes a text from 2 Maccabees 3:34: two men appeared *(ephanēsan)* to Heliodorus, delivered a message to him, and then suddenly, the narrative tells us, became invisible *(aphaneis egenonto)*. The two men are obviously angels. We must understand Luke's account by analogy with that in 2 Maccabees. As though his nature was now similar to that of angels, Jesus is invisible to human eyes. It is in virtue of a divine intervention that he takes human form. And then, all of a sudden, he recovers his heavenly state and again becomes invisible to human sight. We must also understand in the same way the story of Jesus' appearance to the eleven apostles. They are together in a tightly closed room for fear of the Jews, and Jesus suddenly appears to them (John 20:19; cf. Luke 24:36). We must not imagine Jesus crossing the city of Jerusalem and entering the locked room in a more or less magical manner! Jesus was suddenly made visible to the apostles' eyes whereas his risen state kept him invisible.

This is correctly understood by Pierre Masset when he writes in an article[4] which we shall utilize again later on:

> It is fully evident that this risen body is not subject to the servitude of our earthly bodies. But if the Gospel tells us what he is not, it does not in any way tell us what he is. And more especially, this form under which he appears to the disciples, and in which we would love to glimpse—in spite of the laconism of the gospel narratives—some clues to the

[4] Masset, "Immortalité," 334.

nature of risen bodies, this corporeal form seems to be an occasional one that the Risen Christ adopts in order to prove that he is really risen.[5] His is a real form, in no way a hallucinatory one (he allows himself to be touched, he eats with the disciples) but an occasional one in the sense that it has no other goal than to build his disciples' faith; and this is why this visible form does not subsist in the intervals between the appearances. Nothing here gives us any information at all on the habitual status, on the form, of risen bodies.

Therefore, the Risen Christ appears to the disciples under a corporeal form, but it is an "imaginary" form. We can compare the stories of the appearances with that related in Genesis 18. In the company of two angels, God appears to Abraham under a human form. Abraham washes their feet (18:4), readies for them a hearty meal which they eat with appetite (18:6-8). And yet, God and the angels could not be seen by human eyes, they could not eat like humans! They appeared in human form obviously in virtue of a divine intervention making this phenomenon possible. The same holds true for the appearances of the Risen Christ; by his resurrection he belongs to the world of the divine, not to that of earthly realities.

e) This being the case, we are freer to understand the realism of some of these appearance stories. As is true of many gospel stories, we are not obliged to believe all the details, among which some were imagined for a precise purpose. Let us take the case of Christ's appearance to the eleven, told by Luke (24:36-43) and John (20:19-20). There is no doubt that Luke and John recount the same event, which they took from the same source.[6] John's account is much simpler: Christ

[5] Masset writes in a note, "The appearances of the Risen Christ are indeed the only proof of the resurrection for the disciples. They were not the witnesses of the resurrection itself as one would be the witness of an event. They are the witnesses of the Risen Christ."

[6] Many authors believe that Luke and John drew from the same source to write their accounts of the passion and resurrection. See Boismard, *Marc*, 193.

suddenly stands amidst the eleven; he shows them his hands and his side to make himself known; and the narrative ends by mentioning the joy of the disciples. Luke's is much more detailed: first he notes that the disciples believed they saw a "spirit"; this causes a discussion among them which Christ takes notice of. Then, as in John, he shows them his wounds so that they will recognize him; also, he asks them to touch him to prove that he is not a pure spirit. Better still, as they are not yet convinced, he eats in their presence a piece of fish that they give him at his asking. It is possible to hypothesize that Luke added all these particulars to his source with an apologetic intention, in reaction against some Christians who interpreted Christ's victory over death in a purely Platonic sense, that is, believed that only Christ's spirit, his soul, would have escaped death.

This analysis of the appearances of the Risen Christ is not as negative as one might think. Of course, the stories themselves teach us nothing about the nature of the Risen One, as Masset remarked, but the way in which the early Church alluded to these appearances teaches us that people understood—probably later on—that Jesus was beyond the limits of human nature because he had become "heavenly" in nature, resplendent as light.

CONCLUSION

Conclusion

At the end of these analyses, we are in a position to draw some conclusions concerning our victory over death according to biblical revelation.

The Fact and Manner of Our Victory Over Death

From what precedes we have learned that biblical revelation proposes at least three solutions to explain how our victory over death is effected. The first solution sees our victory over death as a *resurrection*. This was adopted by the prophet Daniel, the author of 2 Maccabees, Paul in 1 Thessalonians and 1 Corinthians, and by others. This solution presupposes a non-dualistic anthropology which considers human nature in its psychosomatic unity. At death, human beings in their entirety go down to Sheol,[1] where they become unsubstantial shades, practically lifeless, waiting for the day when God will raise the righteous (and them only) by giving back to them the physical elements necessary to their psychic life and at the same time the vital breath.

---

[1] According to a more radical conception, which could well be Daniel's, humans return purely and simply to the dust from which they were taken.

The second solution, found in the book of Wisdom, pre-supposes a Platonic dualism in which human nature is made up of a soul and a body. At death, only the body disintegrates in the earth while the soul continues to live with God. In their soul, principle of their personality and the whole of their psychic life, humans are therefore *immortal*.[2] But the author of Wisdom wanted to blend Platonism, which it fundamentally adopts, and the solution inherited from Daniel: the soul is immortal indeed, but instead of immediately attaining its final destiny, it must first go down to Sheol. Thus, all souls are assembled in Sheol while waiting for the day when God will come to separate them. The souls of sinners will be left where they are and those of the righteous will be drawn close to God where they will obtain their bliss.

In 2 Corinthians, Paul also blends Platonism and Semitic realism, but in a different way. Human nature is made up of soul and body. At death, the soul leaves the "earthly" body to go and join Christ, with whom it lives in bliss. In this sense, humans are *immortal;* and as soon as it arrives in heaven, the soul finds a new body awaiting it, a body which is not made of earth but is "glorious." Humans then become luminous beings, similar to the stars of the sky. It seems that this was also the position of Jesus, although he expressed himself less clearly on the nature of beatified humans.

Some will want to find a fourth solution proposed in the New Testament tradition. Whether in the Synoptics or John's Gospel, a theme was added to Jesus' teaching—which held to the immortality of the soul—that of the resurrection "at the end of time" (John). Consequently, there would be a gospel foundation to the belief held rather widely today. At death, the soul goes either to heaven or to hell, and it is only at the end of time, when Christ returns, that it will be reunited to its risen body. However, let us note that neither in John nor in the Synoptics do the words attributed to Christ say that it will be a resurrection of *the body*. As in Daniel, it is the "dead" who will be raised, "body and soul" as we would say today.

---

[2] In virtue of a gift from God and not by nature as Plato thought.

Therefore, we are faced with the following fact. Biblical revelation teaches us with certainty the *fact* of our victory over death. But it is divided on the *how* of this victory. It is interesting to note in particular that Paul adapts his teaching to the mentality of his addressees, first Jews, then pagans of Greek culture. We may conclude that the manner of our victory over death is not an object of revelation but remains an open question. We have here a problem that is no longer in the domain of exegesis but in that of philosophy or, if one prefers, in that of theology since theology's purpose is to explain the revealed data by means of a specific philosophy. This is what Pierre Masset recognizes in the article quoted in the previous chapter,[3] "The problem [of the how of our victory over death] is extremely complex. In our opinion it is primarily a philosophical problem."

A Few Philosophical Reflections

As I myself am not a philosopher, I shall liberally quote from Masset's article. It is interesting to observe that he came to adopt the idea of a resurrection happening immediately after our death purely by philosophical intuition, without knowing that his option had solid support in the New Testament.

a) We must recognize that from the point of view of revelation, the best attested solution is the one proposed by Jesus and by Paul in 2 Corinthians. We reach our definitive state immediately after death without having to wait to the end of time to join a body. Many theologians will welcome such a solution because it will free them from having to face a vexing difficulty. For the traditional solution does present a major problem lucidly presented by Masset (p. 332):

> From the philosophical point of view, only this second position [immediate resurrection] seems acceptable. The thesis of the "separated soul," such as the Middle Ages professed,

[3] Masset, "Immortalité," 332.

and generally all that threatens the integrity of the human subject is unacceptable. The extenuated state of the "separated soul" is tantamount to a real amputation of the human being. It is a bad way of stating the problem to ask at what time the body is given back to the soul, as though they were two separate substances independent of one another and capable of existing either together or separately. There is no such thing as either a human being without a body or a human body without a soul. Therefore, it is the whole human being who at the moment of death accedes to eternity, whatever the "glorification" of the body at the end of time might be, as we shall examine later on.

b) But how must this problem of the body be resolved? It is certain that we shall not be joined again to the corpse that was buried in the earth. Paul had strongly affirmed this in 1 Corinthians 15:37-38. Although he still speaks from the point of view of the "resurrection," he explains that what is raised is different from what was "sown." Again, let us quote Masset (p. 333), who saw the problem[4] very clearly:

> It is not the corpse which is called back to life. As soon as the soul has ceased to inform and animate it, there is nothing human about it; it is no longer a human body but a collection of cells in the process of decomposition and reentry into the nitrogen cycle.

And farther on, Masset underlines, very rightly, the fact that biblical revelation does not speak of resurrection of the body but of resurrection of the dead.

c) This negative aspect of the question being accepted, it remains for us to answer the following query: "But if the risen body, the body of the world beyond, is not the same as our earthly body, how must we conceive of it?"[5] Here we must distance ourselves from Platonic dualism. But how and how much? After having described Platonic dualism, Claude

---

[4] We quote only Masset, but today this point is rather commonly accepted by theologians.

[5] Masset, "Immortalité," 333.

Tresmontant[6] presents human nature according to Aristotle and Thomas Aquinas:

> Aristotelian and Thomistic metaphysics teaches that the "body" is a point of view on this concrete reality that the living human being is, its "matter" which is distinguished from its "form" (the soul) only by an abstract analysis. In other words, "body" and "matter" are not *physical* concepts, but *metaphysical* notions proceeding from a metaphysically structured analysis of the concrete reality.

But in this case, how can we justify that humans can continue living while their "matter" is decaying in the earth? Masset's disquisitions are more nuanced (pp. 334–336). What matters above all else is "the human being," "the human subject." Created by God first "in a state of temporal existence,"[7] the human being will be placed "in a state of eternity" only after death. If one wants to keep the notions of soul and body, they must be clarified, purified:

> On the empirical plane of our concrete existence, the word *soul* receives a new meaning: it designates the human subject as the spiritual pole in contradistinction to the material pole called *body,* the immanent principle of information and unification of our material body . . . (p. 335). [But we must consent to affirm that] the body has no other being than the being of the soul, than the being the soul is (in the sense of subject). The body is the phenomenon of the soul, the face with which the soul appears when it is immersed in the world of matter. Not something else, not another substance. But that by which the subject is in the world, that by which the subject has a grasp on the spatio-temporal world and receives from it. It is the empirical equipment of the human subject in view of existence (pp. 335–336).

At death, we shall pass from the world of experience to a totally different world, from the temporal state to the state of

---

[6] Tresmontant, *Essai,* 88.

[7] Which must be considered a "trial" through which we must respond by love to God's plan of love for us.

eternity. We must then say that the body will be the face with which the soul will appear when it finds itself in the state of eternity. There will be a sort of continuity between our body of now and our heavenly body:

> When we shall be in the mode of eternity, beyond the death to this world, our body will subsist, no longer as the phenomenal, spatio-temporal body that death does away with, but as an ontological body, that is, the very being of our corporeity; more concretely, it will be the proper form that—by its functions of individualization, experience, and communication—our empirical body will have contributed, during the course of our existence, to our eternal being. Without this indelible imprint of all that we shall have been, we would be pure spirit. Everything, as far as its eternal being is concerned, will be saved for eternity: everything that made our temporal life—the events of our personal history, our relationships, our thoughts and feelings, our works and memories, everything that we have acquired—everything will be saved, but in its pure essence (p. 336).[8]

d) We are now in a position to answer the question implied in the title of our book: "Must we still speak of resurrection?" Once more, let us quote Masset (p. 337):

> The word *resurrection* is itself an image. It presents the risk of misleading us inasmuch as it evokes the idea of a corpse awakening, coming to life, standing up, and coming out of the tomb.

[8] This is developed by Moingt, "Immortalité," 77–78. He holds that the resurrection of the body will happen only at the end of time: "This resurrection of the external human being, which is the resurrection of the body, is the work of the soul in which the power of the life-giving Spirit is operative. For the soul remains in contact with its historical body through the mediation of the body of Christ, whose roots go deep down into the heart of the physical and human universe. From everything which belongs to the historical body in the one and the other and is destroyed, the soul reconstructs a spiritual body which is the organic network of the connections and junctures with beings and things of which our earthly personality was composed."

Let us not forget that this word originally applied (as in Daniel) to the affirmation of the resurrection of the dead, and not just of the body.[9] Now since, because of its immortal soul, the human being does not die, there is no question of its rising, of its coming back to life. The expression could be understood in terms of Semitic anthropology, according to which the whole human being disappeared, waiting to rise one day. This expression is no longer acceptable if we want to speak accurately.[10] More exactly, as Paul said, we have already been raised. It would be better to speak of *immortality*, but with the added clause that at the end of our earthly life, the soul, thanks to the power of the Spirit which has transformed it, fashions for itself a "glorious," luminous body which is the stamp on the soul of the material, "earthy" body, which the soul has left in the earth and which disappears.

e) But there is a further, essential detail to add. Plato taught that the soul is immortal by nature, in the sense that being immaterial, it does not possess in itself any principle of corruption. Many theologians still accept this. But to understand how the problem of our "immortality" is posed, we must place ourselves on the plane of "existing." The proper name of God is "God Is" (when people speak of God) or "I Am" (when God speaks of God), as was revealed to Moses (Exod 3:14). God identifies the divine being with the fact of existing. But God is the only one who can bear this name. On the contrary, the cosmos is not identified by the fact of existing; it exists only because it shares in the existing of God. God lends it the fact of existing, and should God withdraw it, the cosmos would return to nothingness. This general principle applies

[9] The Apostles' Creed speaks of the "resurrection of the body," but we must understand this last word in the biblical sense, that is, the human being in its totality, inasmuch as it is corruptible (see Gen 6:3).

[10] When the Nicene Creed asks us to believe in the "resurrection of the dead," we must hold on to its essential affirmation, which is that death no longer has any power over us. But the wording is in conformity with the understanding of our victory over death that people commonly held at the period when the Creed was composed.

also to the soul. Whether or not one accepts that the soul is immortal by nature, it can exist only in virtue of a participation in the existing of God. Even though, being immaterial, it does not contain any principle of corruption, this does not mean that it exists by itself; its "existing" can be only a participation in the "existing" of God. If God ceased to "lend" it existence, it would return to nothingness, in spite of its "incorruptibility." Its immortality can only be a gift from God.[11]

The Destiny of the Impious

These last reflections lead us to look once more at the problem of the destiny of evildoers. According to a fair number of New Testament texts, they are doomed to Gehenna, "to the unquenchable fire" (Mark 9:43-48).[12] Today, all agree that this "fire" must be understood in the metaphorical, not literal, sense. It would symbolize the moral suffering to which sinners are subjected, and especially the pain caused by their separation from God. But from the biblical point of view, is this symbolic interpretation the only one possible? No. Most often in the Old Testament, the fire is the symbol of destruction and not of prolonged suffering. This is certain for what we call "Gehenna," a word deriving from the name of the valley where some Hebrews sacrificed their children according to a Canaanite rite by throwing them into a burning furnace in which they were entirely destroyed by fire (see Lev 18:21; Isa 30:33; Jer 7:31-34). But let us limit ourselves to texts from the New Testament. John the Baptist says that the impious will be burned in fire like chaff after the wheat is winnowed (Matt 3:12 and its parallel Luke 3:17). Now the verb used here *(katakaiō)* means "to burn completely," "to consume entirely."[13] The image evokes complete destruction rather than prolonged suffering. The same verb is used by Jesus in the saying concerning the weeds which will be entirely burned when thrown into the fire (Matt 13:40). When

---

[11] See Schillebeeckx, *Church*, 137.
[12] See also Matt 5:22; 7:19.
[13] See Liddell–Scott, *Lexicon*.

he predicts the destruction of the wicked at the coming of the Son of Man, Jesus refers to the Flood and especially to the city of Sodom: "On the day that Lot left Sodom, it rained fire and sulfur from heaven and destroyed all of them–it will be like that on the day that the Son of Man is revealed" (Luke 17:29-30). Indeed, Sodom was entirely destroyed by fire. At the end of this same eschatological discourse, Jesus again alludes to the Flood by saying that "all who live on the face of the whole earth" will not be able to escape the disaster (Luke 21:34-35; see Gen 7:23). Again, it is a complete destruction, by water this time and not by fire. One could adduce other texts speaking of the destruction of the impious, an irremediable destruction, but not of eternal suffering.

In this case, one can think that perhaps Edward Schillebeeckx is right when he rejects the idea of eternal suffering for sinners, but visualizes their fate as a return to nothingness, as a definitive annihilation.[14] God would take back from the wicked the existence "lent" them and they would cease to exist, despite their souls' being "immortal by nature." It would then be necessary to reroute the notion of "judgment" in the direction suggested by Jesus' words in John 3:19-21. The judgment consists in the evildoers' refusing to come to the light. There is divine action of course, but it is motivated by this human refusal. The impious would condemn themselves by refusing God.[15] And it is because they would have rejected God that God would reject them by withdrawing forever their existence which God had lent them.

During their earthly lives, humans reject God by refusing to obey the rules God gave them, laws necessary for life in society (see Mark 7:9; Luke 10:16; John 12:48; 1 Thess 4:8). But it is possible that the final decision, the definitive choice, happens only at the moment of death, when humans "see" what is proposed to them. However, one can well ask whether there really are human beings who hate God to the point of preferring nothingness, or who are proud enough to refuse to be dependent upon God.

[14] Schillebeeckx, *Church*, 136–139.
[15] Ibid., 137.

Near-Death Experiences

Many people wonder: If there is really life after death, why do those who live this new life, especially persons close to us, not give us some sort of "sign" to let us know that there really is such a thing? In other words, rather than trusting the love of God who promises us a blissful eternity, we would prefer the testimony of at least a few "souls" who would tell us what happens "on the other side." But do we perhaps have the witness of quite a large number of persons who came so very close to dying that they experienced in some way a foretaste of what occurs once the big step is taken? It is not as an exegete that we shall bring up the question of what is called "near-death experiences" or "the experiences of those who have had a brush with death." We simply would like to show how, if they were taken seriously, they could illustrate what we have said on the state of the beings who live their immortality in the presence of God.

a) It is only about thirty years ago that people began to show interest in the testimonies of persons who, having barely escaped death, told of their experiences before "coming back to earth."[16] Let us make it very clear at the outset that we are not dealing here with the testimonies of a handful of more or less neurotic individuals, but with those of *millions* of people, who for the most part lived in the United States. In addition, their stories have been collected and analyzed by specialists in psychology and psychiatry, some of whom were most skeptical about the worth of such experiences.

These experiences present five stages, but not all the people who had them reached the last stage. Of the eight million surveyed,[17] sixty percent went through the first stage: they had the impression of coming out of their bodies. Thirty-seven percent arrived at the second stage: they saw their bodies a few yards away; they saw doctors and nurses striv-

---

[16] All the information we shall give on these experiences is taken from Van Eersel, *Source*. See also Kübler-Ross, *Les Derniers;* Moody, *Life* and *Light*.

[17] In 1986.

ing to snatch them from the grip of death by their concentrated care; then they came back to their bodies. Twenty-three percent experienced the third stage: they had the impression of being carried away at a tremendous speed in a long dark tunnel. Sixteen percent went through the fourth stage: they said that after having gone along the darkened tunnel, they reached a world of light, an enormous light, white and golden, impossible to describe; this light was also a radiation of love. Finally, ten percent experienced the fifth stage: they felt that they entered this light; they were part of this light; it was as if they were transformed into this light.

To illustrate the last two stages, here is the testimony of one of those escapees from death. Tom Sawyer, a mechanic, had his chest crushed under the truck he was repairing; he escaped death, although his heart stopped beating in the ambulance which took him away.

> Then, the light began to shine on the horizon. First like a star, then like a sun, an enormous sun, a gigantic sun whose overwhelming radiance did not bother him. On the contrary, it was a pleasure to look at it. . . . Besides–was it possible?–this strange light itself seemed exclusively made of love. The substance "pure love" was all that he could now perceive of the world. And yet he was not drunk. He even had the impression of being more attentive and focused than at any other time in his life. *Life?* Was he not dead?
>
> The more he approached the light, the more the phenomenon increased, and when, finally, he entered it, it was an indescribable ecstasy because then his attention and emotion intensified, he said, "thousands of times." And while an infinity of wondrous landscapes unfolded before him, he understood that he *was* one of these landscapes, that he *was* this huge spruce, that he *was* the wind, that he *was* this silvery river and each of the fish that wriggled in it. Then, and only then, did he remember his whole life (p. 196).

When he was asked for more details on the love he experienced, Sawyer answered: "You see, I am in love with my wife and we have two kids whom I cherish. And yet, all this love taken at its maximum, and even if I should add all the love I felt in my life, all this does not amount to a measurable percentage of what I felt in the presence of the light. A total, infinite love" (p. 197).

b) When one compares these experiences with what we read in the New Testament, one is struck by some coincidences. First, one may wonder if Paul did not have such an experience at least once in his life. In 2 Corinthians 1:9-10, he himself tells us that he was at death's door: "Indeed, we felt that we had received the sentence of death so that we would rely not on ourselves but on God who raises the dead. He who rescued us from so deadly a peril will continue to rescue us. . . ." Here is what he writes in this same letter (12:1-4):

> 1. It is necessary to boast; nothing is to be gained by it, but I will go on to visions and revelations of the Lord.
> 2. I know a person in Christ who fourteen years ago was caught up to the third heaven–whether in the body or out of the body I do not know; God knows.
> 3. And I know that such a person–whether in the body or out of the body I do not know; God knows–
> 4. was caught up into Paradise and heard things that are not to be told, that no mortal is permitted to repeat.

Paul is aware of having in some way left his body behind as in the near-death experiences. He is carried up to the third heaven where he hears ineffable words which no human is permitted to repeat, as in the fourth stage of those experiences.

This comparison can be questioned; in any case, we do not give it more worth than it deserves. More important for us is the theme of light: it dominates the fourth and fifth stages of the experiences. Not only does Tom Sawyer enter a world of light, but he is aware of himself becoming light. Similarly, when Paul is thrown down on the way to Damascus, he is surrounded by light, a light which is Christ himself. When he wants to describe for us the nature of risen beings, he compares them to the luminous splendor of the stars (1 Cor 15:40-42). The whole eschatological world is transformed into "glory" (Rom 8:18-23), this glory which is nothing else than the very light of God that transfigures human beings. Likewise, when he depicts the Messianic Jerusalem, the author of Revelation writes, "And the city has no need of sun or moon to shine on it, for the glory of God is its light, and its lamp is the Lamb" (21:23).

And this light is imbued with love; this is the dominant experience of those who are "almost dead." Now John gives us two definitions of God in his first letter: "God is light" (1:5) and "God is love" (4:8, 16).

At the end of our own earthly life, we too will be welcomed by the God who is Light, the God who is Love.

Index of Scripture

Index of Pseudepigrapha

Index of Authors

155